Ian Hyndman

With Jesus

Bethel Publications

Contents

1

No room in the inn

Here in south-eastern Australia, in the foothills of the Victorian Alps, we often watch beautiful sunsets as they flood the western sky with magnificent displays of colour, creating golden edges around the clouds as the sun sinks lower and lower beyond the horizon.

I was recently watching one of these sunsets, and I thought of another sunset, long ago, as the sun set in the west beyond Bethlehem. It was the time of the census, and Mary and Joseph had come to be registered in Joseph's city.

Joseph was desperate to find accommodation, for Mary was showing signs of discomfort. He wondered if she might even have her baby that night. The town was teaming with people, all come to register in the census. But Joseph could find no accommodation, even for a woman in advanced pregnancy. There was only a stable near an inn.

It was not uncommon for travellers who were poor to be excluded from the accommodation houses in time of high demand for accommodation. Of course, no doubt if you had money, you could always get a bed. Money opens all doors, and bribery was just as rife then as it is now.

Poor travellers were forced to share their humble quarters with the animals. Mary and Joseph were amongst these. They were poor. We know they didn't have enough money to pay for a lamb for the sin offering required under the law as an offering after the days of Mary's purification. Instead, they provided a pair of turtle doves or two young pigeons. Turtle doves cost only one seventh the price of a lamb.

Mary and Joseph were accommodated with the animals when Mary's time came for giving birth.

> "She gave birth to her first born son and wrapped him in swaddling cloths, and laid him in a manger, because there was no room for them in the inn". (Luke 2:7)

She laid him in a manger. This was a feeding trough, or stall, from which the cattle and goats fed. No doubt, as every mother does, she cleaned out this bed for her baby and made it as clean and comfortable as possible. So the Son of God, King of kings, Lord of lords, began his life in a cattle trough.

Can we imagine anything more unlikely? But that's the way God often works, and that's the way His Son lived his mortal life of 33 years, with the utmost humility and lowliness.

So Jesus was born, in the most incongruous of places, for there was no room for them in the inn.

No room for Jesus in the inn. How often over the centuries has there been no room for Jesus in the inns and houses and hearts of the people of the world. He was born during the night. When the sun had set that night, it set on a world which, from that night onward, was changed and different. From that night onward, Jesus has been with us, shining forth as a beacon of light and freedom down through the centuries, as the light of the world.

As Jesus lay in the cattle trough, some shepherds just outside Bethlehem were startled by the sudden and unexpected appearance of an angel. They were obviously very frightened:

> "Don't be frightened", said the angel. "I bring you good news of a great joy ... for to you is born today in the city of David a Saviour, who is Christ the Lord ... You will find him wrapped in swaddling cloths and lying in a manger". (Luke 2:10–12)

We are not told what the shepherds thought of this amazing message, but to receive news of the long awaited Messiah's birth, and to be told he was lying in a manger — a cattle trough — must have struck them as incredible!

The Jewish scholar, Edersheim, tells us that these were not ordinary shepherds. They were from the area outside Bethlehem known as Migal

Eder — tower of the flock. This was where Jacob had camped when he reached Bethlehem after Rachel died, just a few miles further back.

> "Israel journeyed on and pitched his tent beyond the tower of Eder". (Genesis 35:21)

At Migal Eder, the flocks for temple worship in Jerusalem were kept. They were looked after by shepherds all the year round. These shepherds who received the message about Jesus were the shepherds from Migal Eder. How appropriate that the sheep they were looking after were to be used as sacrifices at the Temple. Little did these shepherds know that the tiny baby they gazed down at as it blinked up at them from the manger was to be the greatest sacrifice ever provided. All of their sacrificial sheep were but pointers to this greatest of all sacrifices — the Lamb of God.

We don't often think about how God felt on this special night. His Son, His only beloved Son, created by the power of His spirit. What a privilege for Mary! To have been chosen above all the other women of Israel for this special and unique relationship with God, indicates how God regarded her. She had always loved and worshipped her God, and had been chosen by Him to bear His Son.

As she wrapped her brand new baby, Jesus, only minutes old, in swaddling cloths, we can be sure that she prayed to her God, her heart overflowing with joy and thankfulness. Over the past nine months she would have developed a profoundly close relationship with God. As the woman who was bearing God's only Son in her womb, she would have a closer relationship with her Heavenly Father than any other human being. She would have been in fervent prayer to Him during her nine months of pregnancy.

Now, as she nurses her baby in the way of all mothers, she remembers the words of the angel, Gabriel, nine months earlier:

> "You will conceive in your womb and bear a son, and you shall call his name Jesus. He will be great, and will be called the Son of the Most High ... the child to be born will be called holy, the Son of God". (Luke 1:31–32,35)

Nine months later, here she was cuddling him, this promised baby — the only begotten Son of God. No doubt she bent her head over her little son, in silent prayer, and like Hannah before her, committed him to his Father.

Next morning, a new day dawned. It heralded a new era. Little did the people of Bethlehem, or for that matter, the people of the then known world, realise that between sunset and sunrise, a world-changing event had occurred.

The years pass, and we come now to another sunset. Jesus is by now 33 years old. But he is dead. A few hours before the sunset, he died, after an agonising six hours hanging on a cross.

When he was born, thirty-three years earlier, there was no room for him in the inn. Now, in death, there was not even a tomb for him. A kindly Joseph of Arimathea allowed him to use his tomb. It had never been used before. Joseph had bought it for the use of his family and himself. Had Joseph not made his tomb available, Jesus' body would have been thrown into the Valley of Gehenna, where the bodies of all crucified victims were thrown.

It was Joseph and Nicodemus, accompanied by faithful Mary Magdalene and Mary, the wife of Cleopas, who carried Jesus' body to the tomb.

As they did so, the sun was about to set, marking the beginning of the Sabbath. The men quickly wrapped Jesus' body in linen cloths. The heart-broken women watched as they did so. They placed about a hundred pounds' weight of myrrh and aloes amongst the linen cloths.

So the sun set on a scene of grief and shock. To the disciples, to Jesus' family, to the hundreds, thousands, he had healed, to all of his followers, it was a disaster.

The darkness of night descended. Jesus, who had no home to be born into, had died homeless. Even in his death, his tomb was not his own. It was a sunset of much sadness and mourning.

Then on the third day after his death, the dawn of new day revealed a situation which nobody could at first grasp. Thirty-three years earlier, the dawn of the day of Jesus' birth ushered in a new era. Now another dawn ushered in a miracle which has never been equalled.

In the early morning of the third day, several women made their way through the streets of Jerusalem towards the tomb. It was still dark, not yet dawn. But something had happened long before the women arrived at the tomb. In the dark of night, a new birth had occurred. Thirty-three years earlier, in the dark of night, another new birth had occurred. But this new life in the tomb was different. This was birth *from death*. It took place, not in a stable but in a tomb.

God didn't use any human being to be involved with **this** event. Mary had had the enormous privilege of bringing God's Son into the world. But in raising His Son to new life, God acted alone.

By the time the women stood at the tomb, wondering how the stone had been rolled away, dawn was breaking. This was a dawn never to be forgotten by any of these women. Or by Peter or John, who Mary ran and fetched and who raced down in the first light of day to the tomb to see what had happened.

Dawn, on more than one occasion, has brought good tidings to women. The dawn in Bethlehem found Mary thrilled with her new baby, thankful to God for his safe arrival. A dawn which proved to all (although they didn't know it at the time) that God had chosen this young girl, Mary, to be the mother of His Son.

Now, thirty-three years later, in the dawn of this spectacularly miraculous day, it is again the women who are favoured. Not the men. The angels didn't even appear to them when they entered the tomb. But they appeared to, and spoke to, the women. "Why do you seek the living among the dead?" Then the men came and went into the tomb, but saw no-one.

Minutes later, after Peter and John had gone home, Mary, weeping, looked inside the tomb and saw and spoke to the same two angels as had appeared to the other women a little earlier, probably while Mary was running to fetch Peter and John.

Thirty-three years earlier, Elizabeth had greeted Mary with the excited words, "Blessed are you among women, and blessed is the fruit of your womb". Equally we could say, "Blessed were those faithful women on the dawn of that mighty day of resurrection", who were the first to be told of Jesus' resurrection. And Mary Magdalene was blessed above all the others, because she saw and spoke to her risen Lord before anyone else. She was the first.

In all of these wonderful events, we have a cameo of our life in Christ. When the sun set over Bethlehem on the night Jesus was born, Joseph and Mary were stressed and troubled and anxious as they sought fruitlessly for somewhere to stay for the night. God did not provide them with a comfortable bed with an ensuite attached, with carpets on the floor and hot and cold running water. He directed them to a stable beneath or beside an inn.

The sunset of the day of crucifixion brought unimaginable suffering to those who loved Jesus, as they watched his agonized hours on the cross. For six hours, they had watched helplessly as Jesus struggled and writhed in an effort to breathe, as he bore the fearful agony of crucifixion. The sun set on a scene of death, grief, shock, disbelief.

Dawn always follows sunsets. The darkness always gives way to the light and radiance of dawn. We know there is a spiritual dawn ahead which will banish the night of mortal darkness for ever.

As we wait in our present darkness of night for the dawn of that new day, we remember the dark night of long ago when there was no room for Jesus in the inn. In these last days of night as we wait for him to come again, let us be sure that there is room for him in the inn of our heart. "Behold I stand at the door and knock. If anyone hears my voice and opens the door, I will come in to him ..." (Revelation 3:20).

Jesus himself gave us a warning — a warning to be ready the moment we are called to go to him when he returns.

> "Let your loins be girded and your lamps burning, and be like men who are waiting for their Master to come home from the marriage feast, so that they may open to him *at once* when he comes and knocks" (Luke 12:35–36)

Long ago, shepherds came to his manger and worshipped him. It was night when they came. In the light of new dawn they reflected with joy that they had been the first to worship a new King — the Messiah.

It is night for us, too. But it will not be long before, in the light of new dawn, we, too, will see him, as they did. Our King is coming, not as a baby born in a cattle trough, but from heaven, with radiant power and great glory to take us unto himself.

2

The journey to the king

The wise men who came to see and worship Jesus, had travelled far. They came to worship he "who had been born King of the Jews".

These wise men typified us on our journey through life, and in a sense, represented us. For our journey through life has one overriding objective — to see and worship he who was born King of the Jews.

In our journey across the desert of life, we spread out across the desert through the week, all travelling in the same direction, but on our separate paths. We are always conscious of each other, and anxious about each other's well-being. Sometimes we see each other as our paths cross each other's routes, but although on separate paths, we are always travelling in the same direction.

Each Sunday, we all come in from our individual paths across the desert of life, to an oasis when we remember him in bread and wine, where we pray together, worship together, and consider and remember the King we are travelling to see and worship. At these Sunday mileposts, this oasis, we pause for a while to re-focus our vision on the star we are following, and to strengthen each other for the ongoing journey in the week to come.

The wise men who came on their journey, came from the east, far across the desert on their camels, to find and worship one who had been born King of the Jews. In scriptural terms, "the east" means Mesopotamia, and we can therefore be sure that these men came from Babylonia.

Tradition tells us that there were three wise men. We know well the Christmas carol, "We three kings of Orient are", but as we know, there were not necessarily three of them, and they certainly were not kings. They were wise men, and the wise men of the east were almost always astrologers — magi, from an old Persian word "magav".

They didn't even come at the birth of Jesus. Jesus was about two years old when they arrived at Jerusalem searching for him. There were therefore about two years between the shepherds' visit to Jesus and the visit of the wise men.

Their visit gives us a picture of an unknown number of astrologers who had travelled a long, hard journey through the desert from Babylonia, arriving at Jerusalem and asking, "Where is he who has been born King of the Jews?"

The very presence of these magi seeking for Jesus raises a number of questions:

1. How would gentile astrologers from Babylonia know anything about the birth of a Jewish King?

2. Why would they *want* to worship a *Jewish* king? Nobody from Babylonia had ever before wanted to worship a Jewish king — even in the years of the kings of Judah and Israel. In fact, it had been Nebuchadnezzar of Babylon who had overthrown the Jewish kings and plundered the Jewish Temple and taken captive the Jewish people. Babylon had certainly never worshipped any Jewish king. Why now?

3. The third question relates to the star these men said they had followed. What star? How did they know to follow a star? Where was it now? Was it *really* a star?

Many years earlier, a singular event had occurred in Babylonia when Nebuchadnezzar had appointed a new head, a chief prefect, over his astrologers or wise men. He was a Jew. His name was Daniel. Let's pause for a moment and leave these wise men asking their questions in Jerusalem about the King of the Jews while we consider Daniel for a few minutes.

When Nebuchadnezzar besieged and captured Jerusalem, he told his chief eunuch, a man called Ashpenez, to bring some of the young men of Israel to Babylon. These were not to be ordinary, run-of-the-mill young men. They were to be of royal blood or of high Jewish nobility.

They were to be of the very best appearance and intelligence. They were to be educated and wise. They were to be trained as elite and special advisors to King Nebuchadnezzar himself. They would receive three years' special education and training in Babylon and would learn the literature and language of the Chaldeans.

Amongst these hand-picked young men, who would have been in their mid to late teens, were Daniel, Hananiah, Mishael and Azariah. All of them were from the tribe of Judah, and Josephus tells us that they were of the royal family of King Zedekiah. Daniel and his companions were therefore of royal blood.

Daniel lived in Babylon for between sixty and seventy years. In that time, he had significant and major influence on the kings of Babylon. He was man of great faithfulness to the Lord his God and refused to compromise his beliefs and practices to conform to the heathen practices of Babylon.

No doubt, he also influenced many of the astrologers under his command when they saw the power and influence of the Jewish God, Yahweh, and many turned away from their worship of the sun and stars and became believers in the God of Israel, as did King Nebuchadnezzar himself. Such was the influence of Daniel.

Let's now return to the wise men in Jerusalem. They had in their possession the writings of Daniel, the former revered and respected chief astrologer of about five hundred years earlier. They would therefore know about his prophecy of an anointed one, a prince, a messiah, who was to be born as a Jew. From Daniel's writings, (eg Daniel 9:24–26) they knew that he was to be born four hundred and eighty three years after Daniel's prophecy. So they knew *when* to look for the birth of this King.

But Daniel had said nothing about the birth of the King being associated with a star or brilliance in the sky. For this clue, they had to turn to another Babylonian astrologer, Balaam, who had lived in Pethor in Mesopotamia. When Balaam had been requested by the King of Moab to curse the Israelites, he had been forced by God to bless them, and in blessing them, he had issued some Messianic prophecies. One is particular is found in Numbers 24:17:

> "I see him, but not now; I behold him, but not near. A star shall come out of Jacob, a sceptre shall rise out of Israel ... "

So the wise men of Jesus' day knew that the anointed one would be a person of royalty — "a scepter shall rise out of Israel ... ". There was also the hint of a star to arise. They told Herod, "We have seen his star in the east and have come to worship him".

This star was no natural star:

1. The star is described as "his" star. It was the Messiah's personal star in a way not true of any other star.

2. The star appeared and disappeared on at least two different occasions.

3. It moved from east to west, then from north to south. It had disappeared after travelling west towards Jerusalem, but now, as they left Jerusalem, there it was again, travelling south.

4. It literally came down and hovered over one particular house in Bethlehem. No ordinary star could possibly have hovered over a single house.

Was this star the Shekinah glory of God? The same Shekinah glory which led the Children of Israel through the wilderness? Very likely it was.

So the wise men found the child they were seeking — the one Daniel and Balaam had written about centuries earlier. He was about two years old. No longer living at an inn, but in a house in Bethlehem with Joseph and Mary.

Two years earlier, Jewish shepherds had come to worship the new-born Messiah. Now these wise men from far off Babylonia came to worship him. They were the first recorded gentiles to worship the Messiah. First, the Jews, second, the gentiles.

That is the appropriate order, for we, as gentiles, have been grafted into the natural olive tree of Israel. It was therefore appropriate that the gentile wise men should have been the second group to come and worship the Messiah, and that the Jewish shepherds came first.

The wise men travelled long and far, through blinding desert storms, through fierce and unrelenting desert heat, through country occupied by thieves and bandits. They were strangers and pilgrims travelling to the Kingdom of the Lord Jesus Christ, child though he then was. But they kept on, bearing their gifts of love over all the long weary miles of desert from Babylonia. Obediently, they followed the star, steadfastly, day after day.

They represented us, fellow gentiles. They were the first of millions of gentiles to come to Jesus. Like them, we are strangers and pilgrims on life's journey to the Kingdom of God. Their gentile search for Jesus bears out the wonderful promises to Abraham, "I have made you the father of a multitude of nations". Paul develops this into "If you are Christ's, then you are Abraham's seed, and heirs according to the promise" (Jew and Gentile).

The gentile wise men from Babylonia recognised this. They came from a far country to worship a Jewish King.

It will not be long before the whole world will come to worship him at Jerusalem. Every year they will flock to worship him at Mt. Zion. We are going to him, too. Like the wise men, we know that he will there at the end of our journey through life. But, also like the wise men, we are comforted and strengthened every day as we follow his star. It leads us resolutely on, not to Bethlehem, but to Jerusalem, the city of the great king.

As we follow his star, we carry our gifts for him — gifts of love and obedience. The star we follow is not an ordinary star. It is the bright morning star. Jesus sent us this message about himself in the words of his Revelation:

> "I am the root and offspring of David, the bright morning star"
> (Revelation 22:16)

This is the star which has risen out of Jacob and which we follow, as the wise men did. With them, we follow the star, not looking behind, but always ahead, and onwards, for that is where the star is leading us.

Soon, our journey will be over. Soon, we will meet the King, in his dazzling majesty of power and great glory. As the wise men did, we, too, will fall down and worship him. Just as the Babylonian wise men opened their treasures, we will open the treasures of our hearts and offer him the gifts of love and obedience we have brought.

Our King will recognise those gifts of love and obedience, for these are the very gifts he has given us already. As we pause in our oasis of remembrance week by week, we remember that his gifts of love and obedience were given to us many years ago as he hung on a cross.

That is why he will recognise them again, when we offer them to him, as our gifts to our King.

As we prepare to leave our oasis to resume our journey, let us take with us the lovely words of a hymn by Catherine Morgan:

> "Go before to guide and cheer us,
> Rouse our spirit, speed the race,
> Make us feel thy presence near us,
> Strengthened by Thy heavenly grace.
> When the morning star shall waken
> Gentile lands from darkest night,
> May dawn find us true, unshaken,
> Fit to share its glorious light."

3

The well of Jacob

We find Jesus and his disciples in Judea, where his disciples were baptising a great many people. They were even baptizing more people than John the Baptist at the time, and word came to Jesus that the Pharisees were concerned at the impact Jesus was having on the people. More and more were coming to his disciples for baptism.

Jesus decided to leave this hot spot in Judea and go to Galilee. He and his disciples faced a journey of about seventy miles. Their journey took them through the hills of Judea, and the way would have involved strenuous walking.

About half way through the journey, they arrived at Sychar, in Samaria. John records that,

> "Jesus, wearied as he was with his journey, sat down beside the well. It was about the sixth hour" (midday) (John 4:6)

This was no chance visit to Sychar. The old name for Sychar was Shechem, rich in biblical history. Abraham came to Shechem; Joseph is buried there. Today, it is named Nablus, the scene of much bloodshed in these last days before Jesus' return.

Jesus had come to Sychar for a specific purpose. So important was this purpose that John devotes almost three quarters of chapter four to it. In summary, John tells us:

- This well at which Jesus sat down in weariness was near the field Jacob gave to Joseph. The well was known as "Jacob's well".

- A woman comes to the well at midday — an unusual time to come. The women normally drew water in the morning and evening, not at midday. We don't know the woman's name, only that she is a woman of Samaria.
- Jesus talks to the woman and, leaving her water jar, she runs into the city to tell her townsfolk about Jesus.
- Many of them come out to the well to see and talk to Jesus, and persuaded him to stay with them for two days. They are astounded by what he told them.

Now, to understand the purpose of Jesus in coming to Sychar, and to this well in particular, we need to remind ourselves of the history behind the well. We will leave Jesus talking to the woman beside the well and turn our minds back to when Jacob first dug the well, about eighteen hundred years earlier. We will return to Jesus and the woman a little later.

Let's first identify this well in Jacob's time. We'll quickly establish our facts from two passages of scripture.

First:

> "Jacob came safely to the city of Shechem, which is in the land of Canaan, on his way from Paddan-aram, and he camped before the city.
>
> And from the sons of Hamor, Shechem's father, he bought for a hundred pieces of money the piece of land on which he had pitched his tent." (Genesis 33:18–19)

And second:

> "The bones of Joseph which the people of Israel brought up from Egypt were buried at Shechem, in the portion of ground which Jacob bought from the sons of Hamor the father of Shechem for a hundred pieces of money; it became an inheritance of the descendants of Joseph." (Joshua 24:32)

There is actually no mention of the well in these Old Testament passages. It is John who gives us the information that Jacob dug a well there, on the land given to Joseph:

> "So he (Jesus) came to a city of Samaria, called Sychar, near the field that Jacob gave to his son Joseph. Jacob's well was there ... " (John 4:5–6)

It will be helpful if we go back a little further in history to set the scene for Jacob's time here at Shechem. Jacob had left his parents, Isaac and

Rebekah, some twenty years earlier, when he travelled from Beersheba to Haran to find a wife. On the way, he had spent a night at Bethel where he had a dream, in which he was given the same mighty promises given to his father, Isaac, and grandfather, Abraham. The next morning, he set up a pillar and poured oil on the top of it:

> "So Jacob rose early in the morning, and he took the stone which he had put under his head and set it up for a pillar and poured oil on the top of it. He called the name of that place Bethel ..." (Genesis 28:18–19)

It is important, as we shall see later, to note that he poured oil onto the pillar.

On he went, and over the next twenty years, he married Leah and Rachel and had eleven sons and at least one daughter.

In those years, there was much deceit and trouble in Jacob's life. Jacob came from a family (through his mother) in which deceit was strongly characterised. Jacob himself was deceitful on several occasions throughout his life. He had, with his mother, deceived Isaac in the matter of being given the blessing. Laban deceived Jacob by giving him Leah instead of Rachel for his wife. Laban also deceived him in matters involving sheep and goats, resulting in Jacob leaving Laban secretly with all his family and flocks.

When Laban caught up with Jacob, Rachel deceived Laban by lying to him about the family gods. After Jacob met Esau, Jacob deceived him by telling Esau he would follow him to Seir, when Jacob had no intention of doing anything of the kind. He went instead to Succoth, just near Shechem, and there he bought the land from Hamor's sons and dug his well.

We now join Jacob here at Shechem.

It is of interest to note that there is no mention of Jacob seeking God's guidance in going to Shechem. While he was there, disastrous events occurred. We can see in these events a reflection of human nature and the flesh, for it seems that Jacob had not yet learned to obey God implicitly.

First of all, let's note Genesis 33:14–18, taking up the story from when Esau parted from Jacob:

> "Let my lord (Esau) pass on before his servant, and I will lead on slowly, according to the pace of the cattle ... and according to the pace of the children, until I come to my lord in Seir... So Esau returned that day on his way to Seir.
>
> But Jacob journeyed to Succoth, and built himself a house, and made booths for his cattle; therefore the name of the place is called Succoth.
>
> And Jacob came safely to the city of Shechem ... "

Note that there is no mention of Jacob seeking God's guidance in going to Shechem. In the light of subsequent events, it is unlikely that Jacob had God's blessing in going there.

Not long after arriving at Shechem, Dinah became involved with the young man, Shechem, son of Hamor from whom Jacob had bought his land. Shechem committed fornication with Dinah and her brothers were furious. They planned revenge in a very deceitful way.

They forced the men of Shechem to agree to be circumcised, with the ultimate aim of killing them while they were helpless. But one act of deceit led to another. Here is the deceitful response of the men of Shechem:

> "These men are friendly with us. Let them dwell in the land and trade in it, for behold, the land is large enough for them; let us take their daughters in marriage, and let us give them our daughters. Only on this condition will the men agree to dwell with us, to become one people; that every male among us be circumcised as they are circumcised.
>
> **Will not their cattle, their property and all their their beasts be ours?"** (Genesis 34:21–23)

Because of their sister, Dinah, Jacob's sons killed these men of Shechem. They plundered the city, took their flocks and herds, all their wealth and took captive all the women and children.

Jacob was furious, especially with Simeon and Levi, the ring-leaders in this affair. He never forgot their part in this, and on his death-bed, fifty years later, his words reflected this:

> "Simeon and Levi are brothers; weapons of violence are their swords. O my soul, come not into their council; O my spirit, be not joined to their company; for in their anger they slay men ... Cursed be their anger, for it is fierce, and their wrath, for it is cruel ... " (Genesis 49:5–7)

But Jacob had still not learned to trust in his God. After this bloodshed at Shechem, he said to Simeon and Levi:

"You have brought trouble on me by making me odious to the inhabit-
ants of the land … My numbers are few, and if they gather themselves
against me and attack me, I shall be destroyed, both I and my household."
(Genesis 34:30)

All of this took place where Jacob had dug his well — at Shechem. He
was afraid of what his enemies would now do to him, instead of placing
his trust in God. What had happened to Jacob's faith in God? What did
God's promises, given to him at Bethel, mean to him? This is all the
more surprising when we remember that it was not long before that
Jacob had wrestled with an angel at the ford of the Jabbock River.

All of this smacks very much of fleshly attitudes — attitudes which did
not reflect faith in the God of deliverance and protection. Attitudes
which had deceit and bloodshed as their characteristics.

It is easy to criticise Jacob for this, but it may do us good to examine
our own attitudes, for we, too, fail miserably in our struggle against
attitudes of the flesh and human nature. It seems that for a time, Jacob
had allowed his focus to move away from God. Who among us can say
we have never done that? Let us stay with Jacob a little longer and we
will see that he, as we must, finally turns to his God and is blessed.

As Jacob wallows in fear and self-pity, God steps in. It is as if He says,
"Enough of this, Jacob. Now go and do what I want you to do":

"God said to Jacob, 'Arise, go up to Bethel and dwell there; and make
there an altar to the God who appeared to you when you fled from your
brother Esau'.

So Jacob said to his household and to all who were with him, 'Put away
the foreign gods that are among you, and purify yourselves, and change
your garments; then let us arise and go up to Bethel, that I may make
there an altar to the God who answered me in the day of my distress
and has been with me wherever I have gone'.

So they gave to Jacob all the foreign gods that they had, and the rings
that were in their ears, and Jacob hid them under the oak which was near
Shechem" (Genesis 35:1–4)

In these words, we find a complete change of attitude on Jacob's part. It
appears that he at last realised where his heart and faith should be. He
is going to Bethel, and his mind would go back twenty years to when he
was there before, on his way to Haran.

"Put away the foreign gods that are among you, and purify yourselves, and change your garments". Why hadn't he told his family to put away these gods before? He knew they had them. After Rachel deceived Laban about the gods, he should have got rid of them. After the experience with the angel at the River Jabbock, he should have got rid of them. It is only now that he does.

What great lessons we have here! Not only did they give up their gods, they changed their clothes. It was like a new beginning. We are reminded of the saints in Revelation who washed their robes and made them white in the blood of the Lamb. We have changed our garments and put on the robe of righteousness of Christ Jesus, our Lord. "I will greatly rejoice in the Lord, my soul shall exult in my God. For He has clothed me with the garments of salvation, He has covered me with the robe of righteousness." (Isaiah 61:10).

Jacob buries the foreign gods, and the rings from their ears, under the oak which was near Shechem. Even this had great spiritual significance. This was the oak of Moreh at which Jacob's grandfather, Abraham, camped when he first arrived in Canaan.

On one side of this oak was Mount Gerazim (associated with blessing), and on the other side, Mount Ebal (associated with cursing). Years later, Joshua assembled the Children of Israel at Shechem and told his people exactly as Jacob had told *his* people. "Put away the foreign gods and obey the one true God" (Joshua 24:23).

So Jacob left Shechem, left his well, having put away the things displeasing to God and buried them under the oak there — left them behind, put off his old ways, changed his clothes, left the old ones behind and began his journey anew.

We, too, have left behind our old garments at Shechem and buried them beneath the oak of Moreh. "Be not conformed to this world, but be transformed by the renewal of your mind ... " (Romans 12:2).

Bethel was a couple of days journey from Shechem. Once again, Jacob set up a pillar. This time, he not only poured oil onto it, but also wine, a drink offering (Genesis 35:14). We know from the law, given much later, that the daily sin offering had to include a drink offering — a libation of wine (Exodus 29:36–40). Wine is a symbol of sacrifice and forgiveness.

"Without the shedding of blood there can be no forgiveness of sin."
(Hebrews 9:22)

In this act, we see the growing spiritual maturity of Jacob. He was now close to 100 years old and had lived through many experiences. Now, he had placed his focus on God once more. He had acknowledged his sinfulness before God and sought His forgiveness.

Our thoughts now fly across the centuries, and we return to Sychar, where Jesus is talking to the woman beside the well Jacob had dug centuries before. Jesus is well aware of all that took place here in Jacob's day and has come here with Jacob and the events of his day very much in his mind. But Jesus has someone else in mind, too. He has come here to see and talk to this woman of Samaria. She quickly realises he is a prophet, for he knows all about her and her past and present life.

Then a most unusual thing happens. Jesus tells her that he is the Messiah. This is something Jesus told very few people during his ministry. Now, quite early in his ministry, he chooses to tell this woman, a Samaritan, of all people, and he tells her this momentous fact beside Jacob's well.

The response of the woman was immediate. She left her water jar and excitedly hurried into the city to tell others that she had been talking to the Messiah!

Why did Jesus choose to reveal himself to this woman as the Messiah? Why did he do it at the well of Jacob?

When Jacob first dug this well, his life around the well was reflective of fleshly attitudes, the failings of human nature and sin. Jesus, it is suggested, chose this very place, knowing all that had taken place in Jacob's day, as a contrast between the flesh and the spirit. Between the way of mortality and the way of immortality. Between Mount Gerazim and Mount Ebal. Jacob's well was originally a place surrounded by deceit, violence, weak faith and death. Now, with Jesus beside it, proclaiming life and righteousness, it reflected salvation, forgiveness and eternal life. His presence healed the events of both past and present.

The woman was a person of doubtful moral character. She was living with a man who was not her husband. Why did she come to the well at the sixth hour (midday)? All the other women came in the morning and evening. Maybe the other women disapproved of her way of life and refused to associate with her. By coming at midday, she avoided their critical glances and caustic words. Jesus offered her salvation and life. We remember Jesus' words on another occasion, "I am come to save sinners".

It as if Jesus is saying, "Although this well was originally surrounded by violence, deceit and bloodshed, I am come in the spirit of healing to wipe away the past and replace it with righteousness and peace, and springs of living water which well up to eternal life. The old way of the flesh is gone. I am the new and living way. This woman is a sinner, but I have come to save her and offer her salvation through the water of life which I provide."

Water is a scarce commodity in the Middle-East. Wells were precious. Every day, the women came to get water for their families. This woman had come to get water for her family, but in the excitement of Jesus' message, she had left behind the water of the well, for she had learned of the water of life.

"Whoever drinks of the water that I shall give him will never thirst ... " (John 4:14)

The woman had left behind her water jar, for if we drink of the water of life, we don't need a water jar. The water of life is a spring which wells up to eternal life.

We, too, have talked to Jesus at the well of Jacob. We have accepted the same offer of salvation as Jesus offered to the woman at the well. May we all drink deeply and daily of the words of living water as we listen to Jesus beside the well of living water. May our response be that of the people of Sychar:

"We have heard for ourselves, and we know that this is indeed the Saviour of the world."

4

Are you he who is to come?

"In those days came John the Baptist, preaching in the wilderness of Judea, 'Repent, for the kingdom of heaven is at hand …'"

John the Baptist was an unusual man, to say the least. His birth had been miraculous. Both his parents (Zechariah and Elizabeth) were old when he was born, and Elizabeth had been barren all her life.

It is possible that Zechariah and Elizabeth died when John was a child or a young man. As a young man, John went to live in the wilderness. Some commentators believe he was brought up in the desert by the Essenes. When he was twenty nine or thirty years old, we are told by Luke (3:2–3) that "the word of the Lord came to John… in the wilderness, and he went into all the region about the Jordan, preaching a baptism of repentance for the forgiveness of sins".

He must have presented a strange and compelling spectacle, this austere young man who lived in the wilderness and ate locusts and wild honey. He suddenly appeared out of the wilderness wearing a cloak made of camel's hair and a leather girdle around his waist — exactly the clothes worn by Elijah when he, too, urged the Jews to repent of their sins. Elijah, like John, had also appeared suddenly out of nowhere, as it were, urging King Ahab and the Jews to return to Yahweh, the God of Israel.

John's work was to prepare the way for Jesus. He was, as Isaiah had prophesied,

> "the voice of one crying in the wilderness: prepare the way of the Lord. Make his paths straight." (Isaiah 40:3)

John's message was one of repentance and morality. He was fearless in his denunciation of hypocrisy and immorality. He hurled his message at the Pharisees and Sadducees:

> "You brood of snakes. Who warned you to flee from the wrath to come? Bear fruit that befits repentance and do not presume to say to yourselves, 'We have Abraham as our father ...'" (Luke 3:7–8)

His stinging rebuke did not stop at the Jewish religious leaders. He told King Herod that he had done wrong in marrying his brother's wife. For that, Herod had John thrown into prison in the castle of Machaerus, just east of the Dead Sea, according to Josephus.

The scene now changes, and our thoughts go forward a year or so to a scene in Capernaum. Jesus is there with his disciples, and as was so often the case, Jesus was surrounded by dozens, perhaps hundreds, of sick people — paralytics, those who were lame, blind, deaf, dumb, mentally ill.

Suddenly, pushing through the crowd came two men. They pushed their way to Jesus and told him they were the disciples of John the Baptist. John had sent them to Jesus with a question:

> "Are you he who is to come, or look we for another?" (Matthew 11:3)

Now, this was an extraordinary question from John. Twice, on two consecutive days on the bank of the River Jordan, John had proclaimed of Jesus, "Behold the Lamb of God". No one else, it seems, knew that Jesus must first come as a sacrifice for sin. Everyone, including his disciples, were convinced that Jesus had come as a king to set up God's kingdom there and then. But John called him "the Lamb of God".

John understood that sin and repentance had first to be dealt with. That's why he preached a baptism of repentance. He prepared the way for Jesus as the only way sin could be forgiven. He knew that Jesus came as a Lamb of sacrifice, and that, only after that, would he take up his role as king.

Why did John send his disciples to ask this question?

He knew Jesus was the Son of God. John had been told:

> " 'He on whom you see the Spirit descend and remain, this is he who baptises with the Holy Spirit'. And I have seen and have borne witness that this is the Son of God." (John 1:33–34)

It has often been said that John sent his disciples with this question for their sake, not his. One suspects that this view is held because it would seem unacceptable that John the Baptist had developed doubts about the role and work of Jesus. However, it is entirely possible that John sent his disciples to Jesus with this question, for his own sake.

If this is the case, why did John feel the need to ask the question?

Could it be because John thought things were not going as expected? He had expected a great wave of repentance to sweep Israel. He expected that Jesus would come in judgement on a nation in need of repentance. He had told the crowds just before Jesus began his ministry,

> "His winnowing fork is in his hand, and he will clear the threshing floor and gather his wheat into the granary, but the chaff he will burn with unquenchable fire" (Matthew 3:12)

As John sat in his dank, dark, prison cell, alone and isolated, he heard little of what was going on outside. But from what he did hear, there was no news of a great wave of repentance sweeping the people. There was also no sign that Jesus was about to bear the sins of the people, as the Lamb of God. He had no one to discuss his anxieties with, no one to turn to for re-assurance that Jesus was fulfilling his role as the Lamb of God. It would be natural for one in John's circumstances to wonder if Jesus was going to fulfil this role.

So, he sent word to his disciples to go to Jesus and ask, "Are you he who is to come, or shall we look for another?"

Jesus' response to the question was to show the disciples his tremendous power of healing:

> "In that hour he cured many of diseases and plagues and evil spirits, and on many that were blind he bestowed sight". (Luke 7:21)

And he said to John's disciples:

> "Go and tell John what you have seen and heard … and blessed is he who takes no offense at me". (Luke 7:22–23)

This question of John's stirred Jesus deeply, and his heart reached out to his cousin, this faithful preparer of the way, in his lonely prison cell. He understood John's dilemma and doubts, and we read of Jesus response in the whole of Matthew 11, for in its entirety, it relates to John the Baptist and stands as a mighty testimony of Jesus' love for John.

First, though, he wanted to send John an answer to his question. John needed re-assurance that Jesus was the Son of God and the Saviour of the world. John's disciples watched in amazement and awe as Jesus gave sight to blind people who had never seen the light of day, who had never seen colour or the soft beauty of a sunset. For the first time, they were able to see the person who spoke to them.

He lifted up those who could not walk so that they sprang up and walked for the first time in their lives. He healed those with leprosy. He opened the ears of those who had never heard the voices of others, who had never heard the rustle of the wind in the trees, or the lapping of the waves on the shore of the Sea of Galilee, or the sound of their footsteps in the dusty road. He cured those afflicted with mental illness and calmed their tortured minds.

John's disciples were told that Jesus had raised to life a young man who had died at Nain, only days before, and they heard that the good news of the Kingdom was preached to the poor.

"Go and tell John what you have seen and heard", said Jesus to John's disciples. They had seen the power of the Holy Spirit used by the Son of God. In this, perhaps, Jesus intended to remind John of those beautiful words of Isaiah 35:5–6:

> "Then the eyes of the blind shall be opened, and the ears of the deaf unstopped; then shall the lame man leap like a hart, and the tongue of the dumb sing for joy ... "

Jesus wanted John to know that whilst Jesus' work was primarily one of providing a way in which sin could be forgiven, the people had first to be reminded that their infirmities were often the result of sin. "Go and sin no more" was Jesus' frequent injunction to those he healed. He also wanted to assure John that he was indeed the Son of God, because no one could use God's healing power as Jesus did if he were not God's Son.

John had already witnessed God's spirit descend from heaven as a dove and rest on Jesus as he rose from the waters of baptism. He had heard God proclaim,

> "This is my beloved Son with whom I am well pleased". (Matthew 3:16–17)

Now Jesus was reminding John of this demonstration of the spirit, given by God to His Son. It is as if Jesus said, "John, you saw the spirit of my Father descend on me as a dove, proving that I am His Son. That same spirit enables me to heal the sick of their diseases. This is further proof that I am indeed the one who is to come, and there is no other. My Father's spirit is with me".

So John's disciples were sent back to John with this profound message, witnessed by them personally, that Jesus was the Son of God, and the Lamb of God, and all was going to plan.

But Jesus had been deeply stirred by John's question, and he was saddened by John's plight as he languished in Herod's prison. He wanted the crowd who thronged about him to know something of this mighty prophet and preparer of the way, John the Baptist. He began to tell them about him, and we can imagine the awe and rapt attention of those just healed as they listened to Jesus:

> "What did you go out into the wilderness to behold? A reed shaken by the wind? Why then did you go out? To see a man clothed in soft raiment?... Why then did you go out? To see a prophet? Yes, I tell you, and more than a prophet. This is he of whom it is written:
>
> > 'Behold, I send my messenger before my face, who shall prepare the way before thee'.
>
> Truly, I say to you, among those born of women there has risen no one greater than John the Baptist ... " (Matthew 11:7–11)

Jesus knew that John had expected a great wave of repentance to sweep through the towns and cities of Israel. "His winnowing fork is in his hand ...". But it had not happened. Despite the great work Jesus did (and John before him) in preaching repentance, by and large, there were many unmoved by the message of both men, especially the Jewish leaders.

It is with this in mind that Jesus now upbraids the cities in which he has preached repentance and forgiveness of sin — Chorazin, Bethsaida and Capernaum:

> "Then he began to upbraid the cities where most of his mighty works had been done, because they did not repent. 'Woe to you, Chorazin! Woe to you, Bethsaida, for if the mighty works done in you had been done in Tyre and Sidon, they would have repented long ago in sackcloth and ashes ... And you, Capernaum, will you be exalted to heaven? You shall

be brought down to Hades ... I tell you that it shall be more tolerable on the day of judgement for the land of Sodom than for you". (Matthew 11:21–24)

Jesus now prays to his Father, surely with John in mind:

"I thank Thee, Father, Lord of heaven and earth, that Thou hast hidden these things from the wise and understanding and revealed them unto babes ..."

John knew that Jesus came as the Lamb of God, bearing a message of repentance and forgiveness of sins. Most of all, he knew that Jesus' sacrifice as the Lamb of God — God's only beloved Son — would open up the way for sin to be expunged forever, a way which led to eternal life.

Jesus thanked God that these great truths had been revealed to those such as John, who like us all, needed re-assurance that all was well, and that everything was going as planned.

As Jesus' thoughts and heart reached out to John in his need of re-assurance and comfort, surely that beautiful invitation of Jesus which has rung down through the centuries to us today, was uttered with John in mind. Jesus *knew* his need as he suffered day after day in his dark prison cell, *knew* that he laboured under doubt, *knew* that he needed, as we all do, to take Jesus unto himself.

So it was that Jesus cried out to all, but especially with John in mind:

"Come unto me, all who labour and are heavy laden and I will give you rest. Take my yoke upon you and learn from me; for I am gentle and lowly in heart and you will find rest for your souls. For my yoke is easy and my burden is light". (Matthew 11:28–30)

In effect, although Jesus' invitation is to all men and women, he was saying to John in his heart, "John you are not alone. You don't carry your burden alone. I know you are heavy laden and in need of rest and re-assurance. I will give you that rest. Come to me and let me share your load. John, take my yoke and I will help you, and you will find the rest and re-assurance you need so much. For my yoke is easy and my burden is light."

We all need re-assurance at times, as John did. Do we ponder deep in our hearts that things are not going as we thought they would? Here we are, well into the 21st century, and Jesus has not returned. We thought he would have returned by now, just as John thought that all Israel would have turned to Jesus in repentance. But it didn't happen that way.

Are we troubled by the fact that he hasn't yet returned? Are you carrying a load of trouble or sin in your life? Remember the invitation of Jesus, "Come unto me, all who labour and are heavy laden and I will give you rest." All is going to plan and everything is under control.

Each Sunday, as we come together to remember the Lamb of God, who gave his life for us, may each of us find that rest in him which comes from sin forgiven, and from complete trust in him. As we reach out from our prison of mortality, with all its doubts and fears and anxieties, we reach out to Jesus, our Lord, for not only does he offer us rest and re-assurance in our need, but he has also set us free.

5

A woman of the city

The incident involving "a woman of the city" took place in Capernaum. It is recorded in Luke chapter 7. Luke is the only gospel writer who records the incident.

It involves two men and a woman. One of the men was Jesus, and the other a Pharisee whose name was Simon. This event took place in Simon's house.

The woman is simply described as "a sinner". We are not told her name, but if we take note of a few clues, we can work out who she might have been. First, let us see what Luke says about this woman:

> "One of the Pharisees asked (Jesus) to eat with him, and he went into the Pharisee's house and took his place at table. And behold, a woman of the city, who was a sinner, when she learned that he was at table in the Pharisee's house, brought an alabaster flask of ointment, and standing behind him at his feet, weeping, she began to wet his feet with her tears, and wiped them with the hair of her head, and kissed his feet, and anointed them with the ointment." (Luke 7:36–38)

Before we consider the details of this touching incident, a reminder of the background to it may be helpful.

Jesus was in Galilee at this time. He had just been to the city of Nain where he had raised a young man to life as they were carrying him out of the city to bury him. From Nain, Jesus had walked twenty miles to Capernaum, and while there, the disciples of John the Baptist had come to him asking, "Are you he is to come or look we for another?" We are told that in that hour, he cured many of evil diseases and plagues and evil spirits. This is an important point in connection with what took place in the house of Simon the Pharisee.

When John's disciples had left, Jesus spoke with great feeling to the crowds about John, ending with his invitation which has rung down through the centuries to us,

> "Come unto me, all you who labour and are heavy laden, and I will give you rest. Take my yoke and learn of me, for I am gentle and lowly in heart, and you will find rest for your souls. For my yoke is easy and my burden is light". (Matthew 11:28–30)

It is possible, and even probable, that the woman who was a sinner was in the crowd listening to Jesus.

Let us leave her for a moment while we consider the invitation of Simon the Pharisee to Jesus to come into his house for a meal. This invitation apparently came just after Jesus had finished talking to the crowds about John the Baptist.

We are not told what prompted Simon to ask Jesus to his house, but it is certain that it was not because he liked Jesus. Perhaps he saw how popular Jesus was with the people and felt that he, Simon, would make a good fellow of himself in the eyes of the people if he asked Jesus home for a meal. On the other hand, this Pharisee didn't want to look as if he were a follower of Jesus. He wanted it to be seen by Jesus, and others, that he was not one of his disciples.

It was the normal custom in Israel, as a common courtesy, to greet your guests with a kiss. Then a servant came forward and washed the guest's hands and feet by pouring water over them and drying them with a towel. Next, another servant sprinkled the guest with perfumed water, and also sprinkled a fine perfumed oil over the guest's head.

The guest was then taken to the table, which was a wide, long table, but very low — only a few inches or centimetres off the ground. Around this table on three sides were low couches, again, only a few inches off the ground. The couches were about six feet, or two metres, wide. Those at the meal would lie down on their side on these couches, at full length, with their heads towards the table.

Simon the Pharisee offered none of these normal courtesies to Jesus. In Israel, not to offer them was disgraceful and an insult. In Australia, we could compare it to someone arriving at an isolated homestead in Central Australia after a journey of several hours across the desert, and not offering them a cup of tea. Everyone in Simon's house would have noticed with some horror that Jesus had been slighted by this Pharisee.

Word would quickly get about that Simon had treated Jesus badly. Jesus had only just finished speaking to the crowds of people outside, many of whom would still have been milling about Simon's house waiting for Jesus to re-appear. They heard that Simon neither greeted Jesus with a kiss, nor did he ask his servant to wash Jesus' feet, nor did he anoint him with perfume and oil.

Despite this studied insult to Jesus, the meal began with the guests, including Jesus, reclining around the table, heads towards the table and feet away from the table. The door to the room was behind them.

Then a most unusual thing happened; an occurrence which would have been absolutely embarrassing for Simon. A woman entered the room. Bear in mind that the meal was for men only and no woman was permitted in the room. And this woman was no ordinary woman. She was known to be a "woman of the city". By the way Simon the Pharisee said to himself, "If this man were a prophet, he would have known who and what sort of woman this is", it seems clear that the woman had been a prostitute, or at least a loose-living woman, and everyone knew it.

Why did she come into Simon's house? It is very likely that she had been amongst the crowd when John the Baptist's messengers had arrived. It is possible she had been one of those who had been healed of an unclean spirit. An unclean or even sick state of mind had perhaps led her into her sinful way of life.

It is highly likely that the invitation of Jesus, "Come unto me all you who labour and are heavy laden ..." had entered deeply into her heart and she had responded to the invitation. Whether this is so or not, it is certain that this woman had been profoundly and deeply affected by Jesus' message, and having heard of Simon's disgraceful and discourteous attitude towards him, had felt an overwhelming urge to go to him and show her overflowing love for him. The words of the beautiful song, *The Stranger of Galilee* by Mrs. C.H. Morris come to mind.

They could almost have been the words of this woman, as she listened to Jesus in Capernaum, on the shore of the Sea of Galilee:

> "In fancy I stood by the shore one day, of the beautiful, murmuring sea;
> I saw the great crowds as they thronged the way of the Stranger of Galilee;
> I saw how the man who was blind from birth, in a moment was made to see;
> The lame were made whole by the matchless skill of the Stranger of Galilee.
> And I felt I could love him for ever, so gracious and tender was he;
> I claimed him that day as my Saviour, this Stranger of Galilee."

Words and emotions such as these would fill the woman's mind and heart, and when she heard what Simon had done, she could not bear to think that her Saviour was being so ill-treated in Simon's house.

She entered his house uninvited, and took in the scene at a glance. Luke tells us that she went to where Jesus was reclining, and stood behind him, at his feet, weeping. Her tears fell onto his feet and she wiped his feet with her hair, and kissed them, and anointed them with perfumed oil.

It was a most touching and overflowing demonstration of her love for Jesus. She cared nothing for what those about her might think of her. She came into the room uninvited, a room out of bounds for women. She made no apology for what she did. All that mattered to her was that Jesus had suffered and had been hurt at the hands of this Pharisee, and her love for him was such that she wanted to heal the hurt which Jesus must have felt.

After what Jesus had done for her, she couldn't bear to think of him being hurt by Simon the Pharisee. She could show her love in no greater way than to wash his feet with her own tears, and wipe them with her hair, and anoint his feet with the perfume she had brought.

It is particularly interesting to note Simon's response to this demonstration of love. The feelings and devotion of this woman towards Jesus were absolutely ignored by Simon. It is doubtful that he even recognised the significance of what she was doing. Simon's only thought was that Jesus was allowing himself to be **defiled** by the woman. Jesus was allowing this woman, a sinner, to touch him!

Luke records that Simon spoke within himself,

> "This man, if he were a prophet, would have known who and what manner of woman this is that touches him; for she is a sinner". (Luke 7:39)

Simon ignores the woman's weeping, ignores her devotion to Jesus, ignores the anointing of his feet, and could only think of defilement. The obviously sincere and heart-felt devotion of the woman meant nothing to Simon. The knowledge of this woman's past, and that to be *touched* by a sinner meant defilement, were the only factors of consequence to him.

Before we consider Jesus' response to Simon, let us note in passing the lesson that it is not enough to invite Jesus to our homes. We must invite him into our hearts. Each Sunday morning when we gather around the table of the Lord (this same Lord whom this woman loved), we must each answer for ourselves the question, "The Lord is in this house, but is he also in our hearts this morning?"

Simon did not understand Jesus, but Jesus understood Simon. *"Simon, I have something to say to you."*

He proceeded to tell the story of the creditor who had two debtors, who owed five hundred pence and fifty pence respectively, and he forgave them both.

"Tell me, Simon", said Jesus at the end of the little story, "which of these two debtors will love him most?" Simon by now would have been acutely embarrassed at the turn of events, and no doubt had become quite angry. He answered, grudgingly it seems, "I suppose he to whom he forgave most". "You have judged rightly", replied Jesus.

But Jesus was not finished with Simon:

> "Turning toward the woman, he said to Simon, 'Do you see this woman? I entered your house, you gave me no water for my feet, but she has wet my feet with her tears and wiped them with her hair. You gave me no kiss, but from the time I came in, she has not ceased to kiss my feet. You did not anoint my head with oil, but she has anointed my feet with ointment. Therefore, I tell her, her sins, which are many, are forgiven, for she loved much; but he who is forgiven little, loves little." (Luke 7:44–47)

Who was this woman of the city, a sinner? We do not know for certain, but there are two or three clues which indicate that she could have been Mary Magdalene.

First, Simon the Pharisee lived at Capernaum in Galilee. Magdala, Mary's home town, was only about eight miles from Capernaum. Jesus had been some time in Galilee — at Nain, and now Capernaum. This was Mary Magdalene's country, and it is quite conceivable that she was amongst the crowd at Capernaum listening to Jesus talking about John the Baptist.

Second, we are told by Luke in chapter 8 that Mary Magdalene had been healed of seven devils — evil spirits and infirmities (RSV) — by Jesus. We recall that Jesus, just prior to going to Simon's house, had "cured many of diseases and plagues and evil spirits. Was Mary amongst those who had been healed by Jesus?

Third, Mary Magdalene is named amongst those who accompanied Jesus soon after this event, when he travelled through cities and villages preaching the Kingdom of God.

It is just possible, therefore, that this woman was none other than Mary Magdalene who was so close to Jesus from then on, being present even at his death and just after his resurrection.

But let us return to Simon's house for a moment. We have here Simon and the woman — possibly Mary. What a contrast between these two! Simon, a Pharisee, with thoughts only for his status in Jewish society, wanting to gain some credit in the eyes of the people of Capernaum by being seen to invite Jesus to his house for a meal. Simon, studiously insulting Jesus by deliberately not offering him the commonly accepted courtesies always offered to a guest. Completely overlooking the woman's repentance and seeing only that Jesus allowed himself to be defiled when she touched him.

On the other hand, consider the woman. Her abounding love for Jesus was just so obvious. She had heard that Simon had insulted Jesus and could not bear to think that this Stranger of Galilee — stranger to her until that day, perhaps — could be so badly treated. This man who had looked into people's eyes, into the inner recesses of their hearts, and healed them of their diseases, who forgave them their sins. This man who invited all who would hear him to come unto him, and he would give them rest.

In her distress, she cast aside all custom and fear for what people might think, and went to Jesus to make up for what Simon had not done.

This repentant woman could express her love and gratitude for what Jesus had done for her in no more meaningful and personal way than in washing his feet with her tears of compassion and love, and drying them with her hair. Jesus must have felt deeply touched and affected by this outpouring of unashamed love for him.

We can derive an important lesson from these two — Simon and the woman. Each Sunday, we gather together to meet with Jesus at another meal. Do we come with hearts of stone, like Simon did, at his meal with Jesus? Let us not emulate Simon the Pharisee, who invited Jesus into his house, but not into his heart. Let us not be so affected with apathy, cold-heartedness and pre-occupation with what people think of us, when we come to our meal with Jesus each week.

This faithful and loving woman was granted healing and forgiveness by Jesus, and so have we. Our gratitude and love towards the same Jesus as she worshipped must surely be no less than her's. She was not concerned with outward appearance. Have you ever wondered what state her face and hair would have been in after she had been crying, no doubt for quite a while, and wiping Jesus' feet with her hair? Swollen and red eyes and dishevelled, wet hair would not cause her to look her best. But this was of absolutely no consequence to her. All that mattered was her love for Jesus, and that he knew that she loved him.

All of this we remember as we share our meal with him each week. As we do so, may our love be as out-flowing and as deeply felt as the love shown by this woman of the city.

6

Feeding the five thousand

"There is a lad here who has five barley loaves and two fish ..."

We find ourselves on the north-eastern shore of the Sea of Galilee at Bethsaida. Not the Bethsaida where Peter, Andrew and Philip came from. That was on the western shore. The Bethsaida of the north-eastern side of the Sea of Galilee was known as Bethsaida-Julia, named after Julia, the daughter of Caesar.

It is Spring time in Israel; the grass is green and there is lots of it. The sun overhead beams down out of a wide, blue sky onto this beautiful scene very close to where the Jordan River spills into the northern tip of the Sea of Galilee.

Thousands of people are here. In their midst is Jesus of Nazareth and his disciples. A few disciples are moving amongst the crowd, assessing who needs assistance to get closer to Jesus, noting the sick and the lame amongst them, and generally keeping an eye on things.

To understand the context of this great gathering, we need to go back a few days. We find ourselves in King Herod's palace, on the eastern shore of the Dead Sea — forty miles south of Bethsaida Julia. We are there as he celebrates his birthday. In the midst of the drunken coarseness and yelling, sensual birthday orgy, Herod made a promise he had to keep. The horrifying result was that John the Baptist was decapitated, and his head brought to Herod on a platter.

The faithful disciples of John, after burying John's headless body, straight away went to tell Jesus of the death of John. Their journey would have taken a couple of days, from the Dead Sea, north to Galilee.

The news for Jesus and his disciples was devastating. At the time, Jesus was at Capernaum. When the disciples of John reached him with the dreadful news, Jesus was surrounded by people, healing and teaching. It was just after lunch. Mark catches the sense of the scene when he says, "Many were coming and going and they had no leisure even to eat." Jesus and his disciples didn't even have time to have lunch.

We can imagine the effect of the miracles of Jesus on the people around him. They were staggered at his power of healing, and hung on every word of his teaching. Amongst the crowd was a boy of between twelve and fifteen years of age.

Suddenly, the news of John's death changed all this. Jesus and his disciples, deeply grieved at the news of his death, got into a boat and sailed off across the top of the lake. "Come ye apart and rest awhile", Jesus told his disciples. Their objective was obvious to the crowd they left behind — they were headed for Bethsaida Julia.

A few of the crowd began to run. They would go to where he was to land. It was about four miles away. Others followed them, and more and more began to make their way around the northern tip of the lake.

They arrived there before Jesus. Instead of a quiet time of rest and reflection to think about John, Jesus saw in these people who had raced around the lake a great need. He felt deep compassion for them, for they were like sheep without a shepherd. There was an estimated fifteen thousand people there — five thousand men beside women and children, we are told.

The afternoon wore on, and it was now late in the afternoon. "It's late", said his disciples, "send the crowds away to buy food."

"You feed them", replied Jesus, and we know he said it to test their faith in him.

"But", spluttered Philip, "200 denarii would not buy enough bread for each of them to get a little". (A denarius equalled a labourer's wages for a day. 200 denarii equalled 200 days' wages. This gives us an indication of the size of the crowd).

Then Andrew spoke up and said, "There is a lad here who has five barley loaves and two fish, but what are they amongst so many?"

Let's pause a moment to think about this. How did Andrew know about this boy? There was a vast crowd, about fifteen thousand people. How did he know that the lad had five barley loaves and two fish? Andrew's gift was his concern for people. It was Andrew to whom Philip brought the Greeks who had come to see Jesus. Andrew was a people person. Very likely Andrew had noticed this boy and kept an eye on him because he was a mere lad, not much more than a child. It was like Andrew to do that. He had obviously talked to the boy, and probably asked him what he was going to do about something to eat.

Incidentally, there is an implication here that no one else had brought any food with them. If they had, Andrew would not have singled out the food brought by the boy when talking to Jesus. The people had rushed around the lake with no thought of the evening meal. They just had to get to Jesus. There was no thought of food.

One wonders whether we are as keen to "get to Jesus". He was the only focus for these people. Is he our primary focus also?

How old was this "lad"? He was obviously there without his parents, for he had his own food. So he wasn't a small boy. He is described as a lad, so he was not a young man. We can assume, therefore, that he was between about twelve and fifteen years old. He had brought with him five loaves and two fish. Perhaps his mother had made sure he took something with him when he left home that morning. If so, she had provided enough for both lunch and the evening meal, for the loaves and fish were for his evening meal. We note, too, that his loaves were barley loaves. Barley loaves were the cheapest bread available, giving us a clue that this boy was from a poor family.

There is one more thing about this lad which we should note as important. **He was willing to give all the food he had to Andrew and to Jesus.** He had nothing left. A boy of about twelve or fifteen would be hungry by this time of day, but he willingly gave them his food. Our minds go back to the widow of Zarephath when Elijah asked her to give him her only remaining food. She did so, and from then on, God provided a continuing supply of food from her barrel of meal. Likewise, this lad gave all the food he had.

It was no small thing to feed this great multitude. Jesus told the people to sit down on the grass in groups of fifties and hundreds. This meant about two hundred and twenty five groups, some groups of fifty, some a hundred. The disciples were to distribute the food to the people. This would mean that the disciples had to distribute bread and fish to nineteen groups each — an average of twelve hundred and fifty people served by each disciple, if there were fifteen thousand people there This was catering on a large scale!

Matthew tells us that once the people were seated in groups, Jesus "took the five loaves and two fish and looked up to heaven, and blessed, and broke and gave the loaves to the disciples, and the disciples gave them to the crowds".

The noted Scottish Bible commentator, William Barclay, writes of this event:

> "The Jewish grace before meals was very simple: 'Blessed art Thou, Jehovah our God, King of the universe, who brings forth bread from the earth.' That would be the grace which Jesus said, for that was the grace which every Jewish family used".[1]

There is another reason why we can be almost certain that Jesus used this standard Jewish prayer that day. This whole event was designed to show that Jesus was the bread of life, sent from *heaven*. The prayer of thanks for the meal mentions the "bread brought forth from the *earth*".

The very next day, in the synagogue at Capernaum, Jesus brought home this lesson to the people — the same people whom he had fed the previous day, for by now, they had returned to Capernaum. They knew he was in the synagogue, and it does not take much imagination to know that the people would flock to the synagogue to see him again. Jesus told them in the synagogue:

> "Do not labour for the food which perishes, but for the food which endures to eternal life... I am the bread of life; he who comes to me shall not hunger, and he who believes in me shall never thirst." (John 6:27, 35)

The disciples gathered up twelve baskets full of food left over — equal to one for each disciple. Did you notice that as he broke the bread and fishes, he gave them to the disciples and the disciples gave them to the

---

[1] William Barclay, *The Gospel of Matthew*, Vol. 2, The Saint Andrew Press, Edinburgh, 1975, P. 100

people? We find another point of interest in these twelve baskets full of food left over.

The twelve baskets, full of bread and fishes, is perhaps a sign that it was the work of the apostles to spread the gospel of the bread of life after Jesus had ascended to heaven. It was no accident that Jesus stressed again and again the next day that he was not only the bread of life, but that he comes to give eternal life to those who accept him as the bread of life. He comes in stark contrast to the bread from the earth — manna in the wilderness. The manna fed the children of Israel physically, but he, as the bread of life, gives spiritual food:

> "I am the bread of life. Your fathers ate the manna in the wilderness, and they died. This is the bread which comes down from heaven, that a man may eat of it and not die. I am the living bread which came down from heaven; if any one eats of this bread, he will live for ever ..." (John 6:48–51)

This was the essence of the gospel, the new covenant, that the apostles would teach and proclaim after Jesus had departed to heaven.

Before we leave this meal at Bethsaida Julia, there is another fascinating point to note. In John 6:9, the Greek word for "fish" is *opsarion*, which means small (dried or pickled) fish to be eaten with bread.

The Sea of Galilee is rich in these little fishes — like sardines. They were especially known by the fishermen and local people of the Sea of Galilee. Salting and pickling of these fishes was a special industry amongst the fishermen.

With this in mind, it is interesting to read from John 21:9–13:

> "When they (Peter, Thomas, Nathanael, James and John and two other disciples) got out on land, they saw a charcoal fire there, with fish lying on it, and bread. Jesus said to them, 'Bring some of the fish that you have just caught'. So Simon Peter went aboard and hauled the net ashore, full of large fish, a hundred and fifty-three of them; and although there were so many, the net was not torn. Jesus said to them, 'Come and have breakfast' "

The word for the fish lying on the charcoal fire is the same word — *opsarion*. Jesus is cooking these little fishes, and once again the disciples partook of a meal of bread and little fishes.

Is there a lesson to be found here? It is suggested there is a link between the Bethsaida meal and this breakfast on the shore of the Sea of Galilee. Consider these facts:

1. Just after the Bethsaida meal, in the night which followed, Peter began to walk on the sea towards Jesus, but his faith failed, and he began to sink. Jesus immediately put out his hand and caught him.

2. On the night of Jesus' arrest, Peter denied Jesus three times. That was beside a fire in the courtyard of the high priest. After the third vehement denial, the cock crowed, and the Lord turned and looked at Peter. Peter had not known he was there. Jesus had heard Peter's denial of him. It broke Peter's heart.

3. It was Peter, John tells us, who hauled the net ashore full of one hundred and fifty-three fish. A miracle.

Was this breakfast of bread and fishes a message for Peter? In effect, Jesus was saying to Peter, without putting it into actual words:

> "Peter, this meal this morning was the same as we ate at Bethsaida Julia — bread and little fishes. You saw that miracle, but just after that, your faith in me failed.

> Peter, This fire may remind you of your denial of me a few short weeks ago. It was beside a fire that you said you never knew me.

> Peter, I have just shown you once again the power that my Father has given me. You did not catch any fish last night, but I have given you such a large catch you could hardly haul it in."

> "Do you love me, Peter?"

Three times, Peter affirmed his love for his Lord in the crisp dawn of that new day, as the waves lapped the shore of the Sea of Galilee.

Jesus was saying to Peter, "Be strong! Love me no matter what. Trust me, no matter what." It was a new day in Peter's life; the dawn of a new beginning for him. On that day, he affirmed his love and faith in Jesus.

Well, all of this happened a long time ago. But for us, it is as real and as meaningful today as it was then. We must not labour for the bread which perishes, but for the bread which endures to eternal life. Sunday by Sunday, we partake of a meal of life, a meal of never-ending provision. It is a meal which reminds us of the mighty and limitless power of God and the supreme authority with which He has invested Jesus, our Lord.

The people at Bethsaida Julia, we are told, would have made him king there and then. For us, he *is* our king. He feeds us, he heals us, he saves us from sinking beneath the wild waves of life. He meets with us in our own familiar places. He speaks to us in ways we understand. Just as he fed the people at Bethsaida with familiar, simple, local food. He is our bread of life.

What became of the young lad with the five loaves and two fish? He must have been spell-bound at the healing power of Jesus, and at what he told them of the Kingdom of God.

The boy gave everything he had to Jesus. And Jesus repaid his faith and selflessness by using that boy's simple food to feed fifteen thousand people.

We can be confident that the boy became a follower of Jesus after that great experience. One day, this same boy will eat another meal with Jesus — at the marriage supper of the Lamb. Once more, he will be one of a great throng of people worshipping Jesus, and *his* voice will shout amongst *all* the voices:

> **"Hallelujah! For the Lord our God the Almighty reigns. Let us rejoice and give Him the glory, for the marriage of the Lamb has come, and his bride has made herself ready".** (Revelation 19:6–7)

It is our prayer that we, too, will be there with the boy, with Andrew, with Peter and with all the apostles, as we gather together to partake of that greatest of all meals, with him who is, and always will be, *our* Bread of Life.

> "Break thou the bread of life, dear Lord, to me,
> As thou didst break the loaves beside the Sea.
> Beyond the sacred page, I see thee, Lord,
> My spirit pants for thee, O living Word.
> Bless thou the truth revealed this day to me,
> As thou didst bless the bread by Galilee;
> Then shall all bondage cease, all fetters fall,
> And I shall find in thee, my all in all."[2]

---

[2] By Mary Ann Lathbury

7

A gathering storm

On the shore of the Sea of Galilee, evening was coming on.

It had been a busy and stressful day for Jesus. First, his healing of many people at Capernaum. Then came the news of the death of John the Baptist. In his grief, Jesus and his disciples had sought solitude at Bethsaida Julia, on the northern shore of the Sea of Galilee. But the crowds had raced around the top end of the lake and met him there. He taught them, and fed them, bidding them be seated in groups of fifties and hundreds on the grass.

It was now time for them to return to their homes, for Jesus wanted to go up into the hills to commune with his Father. Mark tells us that Jesus "immediately made his disciples get into the boat and go before him to the other side while he dismissed the crowd."

As darkness fell over the Sea of Galilee, the disciples, several of them experienced fishermen and weather experts, would notice with some concern that clouds were gathering and that the water on the lake was choppy. They knew this lake and its weather intimately, and there is a hint here that they may have been reluctant to set out on their journey across the lake. We know from scripture what was to come out on the lake that night, and it is highly probable that their reluctance was based on their observation of the weather. One of the characteristics of the Sea of Galilee was its propensity to be whipped up into a seething cauldron of waves and wind, caused by the winds sweeping down suddenly from the surrounding hills whenever storms were brewing. The disciples were well aware of this danger.

Mark's words, that Jesus *"made his disciples get into the boat"* provide for us the clue that there may have been some reluctance by the disciples to embark on such a journey when the weather signs were so threatening. If so, they would set out with feelings of misgivings and anxiety. Jesus was not with them, for he had gone up into the hills, alone at last, to pray.

In the darkness of the night came the howling wind.

Many years earlier, another much larger multitude of people had stood on the shores of the Red Sea, as storm clouds gathered and the wind rose to a crescendo, whipping up the sea in front of them. Behind them, the Egyptian army raced towards them. They were trapped. There was no escape. It was evening, just as it was at Bethsaida Julia.

As the Children of Israel stood there facing the Red Sea, with growing apprehension and fear, they could see great banks of black clouds gathering and heaping up in the threatening eastern sky, and the wind howled about them.

Back now to the Sea of Galilee, as it was whipped into great waves and turmoil as the disciples battled against a head wind which tossed their little boat around like a cork.

Then in the black darkness, as they battled to keep afloat, they saw a sight which terrified them. They saw Jesus, walking on the wild waves. *He wasn't headed towards them*, in fact, Mark tells us that "he meant to pass by them." Mark also tells us that the disciples thought they were looking at a spirit, for all saw him and were terrified. Matthew writes, "They cried out for fear".

At their cry, Jesus called out to them above the tumult of the wind and waves, "Take heart, it is I; have no fear."

Our thoughts return to that frightened mass of people on the shore of the Red Sea as they stood in the gathering darkness and looked out into the unknown. As they watched and waited, listening to the rising wind and watching the black clouds heaping up; casting fearful glances behind them at the approaching Egyptian army, they, too, cried out in fear:

> "What have you done to us in bringing us out of Egypt? It would have been better for us to serve the Egyptians than to die in the wilderness."

Above the roar of wind and waves, the clearly heard voice of Moses cried out,

"Stand still, and see the salvation of the Lord."

He stretched out his rod, and "the Lord drove the sea back by a strong east wind all night and made the sea dry land, and the waters were divided."

In the black darkness of night, the Children of Israel walked in faith down into the Red Sea, between the mighty walls of water. Not only was that crossing — that baptism, as it were — made in darkness, lit up by the pillar of fire behind them, but they also crossed in the midst of a violent thunderstorm.

Here was fear! But here also was faith! Heading into darkness, with walls of water on both sides of them, lashing rain, the crash of thunder, flashes of lightning all around them:

> "When the waters saw Thee, O God, when the waters saw Thee, they were afraid, yea, the deep trembled. The clouds poured out water; the skies gave forth thunder; Thy arrows flashed on every side. The crash of Thy thunder was in the whirlwind; Thy lightnings lighted up the world; the earth trembled and shook.
>
> Thy way was through the sea, Thy path through the great waters; yet Thy footsteps were unseen. Thou didst lead Thy people like a flock by the hand of Moses and Aaron." (Psalm 77:16–20)

Psalm 77 tells us that the crossing of the Red Sea was performed in the middle of a flashing thunderstorm, in lashing rain, in the pitch black of night, with a pillar of fire between the Children of Israel and the Egyptians.

There was enormous faith displayed by both the Children of Israel and the disciples on these respective nights of darkness. The Children of Israel followed Moses and did as he commanded, regardless of the black and stormy darkness and the towering wall of water on each side of them, as they crossed the Red Sea on dry land.

The disciples, too, in obedience to Jesus, set out on their journey, back across the lake, when their trained weather eye warned them that stormy conditions were blowing up.

It is worth pausing here to note that Jesus "would have passed by them", as he walked on the waves of the Sea of Galilee. He would see that they were in deep trouble, yet he "would have passed by them". It was only when they cried out in fear that he came to them immediately and said, "Take heart, it is I; have no fear."

We see in this an important principle for us to use in our own lives. It is the principle that we must seek out God's presence. God does not come to us if we do not ask Him to. Jesus did not come to the disciples until they cried out in fear. "Behold, I stand at the door and knock", he told the ecclesia at Laodicea. But we must respond to that knock. If we do not open the door, Jesus will pass on over the wild waves of our lives and we will be left to struggle in the morass of life's problems. If we open the door, Jesus will come in. God, and His Son, are always there. They have invited us to come to them, but we must respond to that invitation: "Come unto me, all who labour and are heavy laden, and I will give you rest".

We must all face the storms of life. At the time of writing (2004) we are facing the gathering clouds of terrorism and violence all around the world. It seems that the gathering storm of Islamic militarism is quite outside the competence of world governments to deal with. At this time, Arab and Islamic nations around Israel are seething against the West, especially Israel and America. It is possible that an attack against Israel will come out of this, unleashing a war which will signal the beginning of the "time of great tribulation" spoken of by Jesus. This "storm" will be a testing time for all of God's people, both Jew and Gentile. In the midst of this storm, we must reach out to our God and trust in Him for safe deliverance. "Here is a call for the endurance of the saints, those who keep the commandments of God and the faith of Jesus", wrote Jesus in Revelation 14:12.

We must never forget that the "battle is the Lord's."

On another level, the wild sea of life can often bring its darkness and storms, its fears and its problems. Family problems, personal problems, marriage problems, work problems, ecclesial problems — all can bring despair, anxiety and fear.

In such times, we remember that in the midst of our personal storms, and in the dark of night, Jesus is there, walking beside us on the wild waves, ready to come to us if we call to him. "Take heart", he says. "Have no fear."

Importantly, these words of Jesus take us beyond the problems of this mortal life. We are taken beyond all suffering and anxiety and beyond death itself. This life, looked at in the perspective of immortality in God's Kingdom, is but a fleeting shadow.

We need have no fear of the future if we belong to Christ. He has provided the way to eternal life. If we follow him in obedience and love, we will be with him when he reigns in the wonderful Kingdom of God:

> "He has delivered us from the dominion of darkness and transferred us to the Kingdom of His beloved Son, in whom we have redemption, the forgiveness of sins." (Colossians 1:13)

The darkness of the night, forbidding and frightening though it is, disappears before the radiant sunshine of the dawn to come. As the Children of Israel rejoiced in the dawn after crossing the Red Sea, and as the disciples rejoiced in the dawn after their stormy crossing of the Sea of Galilee, so we will rejoice at the dawn of the day which brings the return of Jesus. For then, our storms will be over, and there will be the joy of the putting off our mortal nature and being granted the new clothing of immortality in a world renewed and shining with the glory of God in its midst.

"Amen. Come Lord Jesus".

8

Jairus: ruler of the synagogue

The synagogue in Capernaum was packed with people who had come to see and hear Jesus of Nazareth speak — this young prophet who had recently come to live amongst them at Capernaum.

He'd only been at Capernaum a few weeks, but already he had brought the people of Capernaum to their feet in wide-eyed amazement. In the process, he had caused rapidly growing concern and alarm to the Jewish religious leaders.

The early chapters of Mark are packed with accounts of the people Jesus healed at Capernaum. In the very first chapter of Mark, we read of a man with an unclean spirit whom Jesus healed. The people in the synagogue were "astonished, for he taught them as one who had authority, and not as the scribes."

We are told that "at once, his fame spread everywhere throughout all the surrounding region of Galilee."

The Jewish leaders were not pleased. Not only had Jesus attracted the attention of the people, but he had healed this man on the Sabbath. On the same day, Jesus healed Peter's mother-in-law of a fever. And that evening, at the end of the Sabbath, crowds of people came clamouring to Peter's door, bringing with them their physically and mentally sick family members. Jesus healed them all. The Jewish authorities grew even more concerned.

A few days later, they heard he had healed a paralytic — a man who was actually let down through the roof of a house by his friends who could not get near Jesus because of the crowds pressing all around him.

Another week or so passed. By this time, the ruler of the Capernaum synagogue had sought the assistance of other Jewish leaders — Pharisees, probably from Jerusalem.

Once again, Jesus entered the synagogue on the Sabbath. This time, the ruler of the synagogue was ready for Jesus. He had with him these Pharisees, and Mark 3:2 tells us that "they watched him, to see whether he would heal again on the Sabbath." There was a man there with a withered hand.

The people were aware of what was going on. It was well known that the ruler of the synagogue had brought his superiors here to deal with this young teacher and healer. They knew the rulers saw him as a threat. But to the people, he brought them something they had never seen before. And he told them of the Kingdom of God and the love of God.

In the front rows of the synagogue sat the pompous scribes and Pharisees, with gimlet eyes, watching Jesus to see whether he would heal anyone on this Sabbath day.

How Jesus despised these men. Only a few short weeks later, he would denounce the Pharisees:

> "Woe to you, for you tithe mint and rue and every herb, and neglect justice and the love of God ... "

> "Woe to you Pharisees! For you love the best seats in the synagogues and salutations in the market places ... " (Luke 11:42–43)

Time and time again in his ministry, Jesus taught by word and example that the Jewish leaders had failed to show compassion and love for their flock. The law and its ritualistic observance had become paramount to them, and justice, mercy and love was not part of their daily ministry as shepherds of the flock of God.

So now, these Pharisees in the synagogue at Capernaum were not the least concerned about the needs of the people. They were concerned only about whether Jesus would break the law of the Sabbath. They watched Jesus to see what he would do. The ruler of the synagogue was there with them.

Jesus knew well their thoughts, and as he entered the synagogue he saw there the man with a withered hand.

"Come and stand here", he said to the man. Mark relates that Jesus looked around at the Pharisees with anger, grieved at their hardness of heart. He said to the man, "Stretch out your hand." And as the man did so, his hand was healed and made whole.

I wonder what the ruler of that synagogue thought about this miraculous incident. Was his heart also hard, like the Pharisees? Was he also filled with fury as they were? Or did the healing of this man's withered hand make him think about Jesus more deeply? Perhaps he wondered in his heart about the way this remarkable young man so blatantly ignored the law of the Sabbath, and other laws, too.

Like the Pharisees in his synagogue that Sabbath day, this ruler had to learn that love and compassion and mercy were missing from his ministry.

It was only a few short weeks later that this same ruler of the synagogue found himself in deep distress. For this ruler was none other than Jairus, whose daughter had become perilously ill. In his plight, he thought about Jesus, how he had healed the man with the withered hand, the paralytic and the man with the unclean spirit. He had no doubt heard how he had healed Peter's mother-in-law of the fever.

Gone now were his scruples about this young man. No longer was he concerned about the jot and tittle of the law. His only thought was that his little daughter was seriously ill and that perhaps Jesus could heal her.

But Jesus had left the district to go over the Sea of Galilee to the country of the Gerasenes. Anxiously Jairus waited for him to return. His daughter grew worse as each day passed. There were no telephones in those days. No way of sending a message to Jesus. Jairus had to wait for him to return.

At last word flashed around Capernaum that Jesus was back. A huge crowd quickly gathered down by the shore, for Luke tells us "they were all waiting for him."

Down rushed Jairus, pushing his way through the milling crowds. When people looked around to see who it was that pushed his way through them, they quickly stood aside to let him pass when they saw it was none other than Jairus, the ruler of the synagogue.

At last he pushed his way through the thronging multitude to where Jesus stood. He flung himself down in desperation at Jesus' feet (a very different Jairus now) and pleaded with him to come with him. "My little daughter is at the point of death. Come, and lay your hands on her, so that she may be made well, and live."

There are two points to note in Jairus' words to Jesus. First, his expression "my *little* daughter" conveys his deep love for his little girl. He could have said, "Come and heal my daughter", but his words contain a more urgent emotional response. This is not the stern, unrelenting ruler of the synagogue, it is a desperate father who cares more than anything in the world about his little daughter.

Second, the healing work of Jesus in the Capernaum synagogue has not gone unnoticed by Jairus. He has seen Jesus lay his hands on others, and heal them, and now asks Jesus to do the same for his daughter. Already, his faith that Jesus can do this is strong. The heart of Jairus has begun to change.

Jesus agrees to go with him, and "a great crowd followed him and thronged about him", writes Mark.

Jairus, having waited for some days for Jesus to return, watching his daughter slowly sinking towards death, would be frantic for Jesus to hurry. But his progress was so slow! He could only make slow headway because of the huge crowd who pressed in on him on all sides. "Hurry", thought Jairus, "before it is too late." Every minute brought the risk of his little girl's death.

Then suddenly, and without warning, Jesus stopped. We can imagine Jairus' utter desperation now. His little daughter, only twelve years old, was at the point of death and Jesus had stopped. What was holding him up?

Then Jairus saw what had caused Jesus to stop. Jesus had said, "Who touched me?" There, on the ground in front of Jesus, was a woman whom Jairus recognised. It was the woman who had been banished from his synagogue twelve years earlier, because she was unclean with an issue of blood.

Let's pause here with Jesus and Jairus for a moment to consider this woman. Her complaint was of a most personal nature. Her bleeding had not stopped for the past twelve years. People in Capernaum would know of her because of her complaint. It had caused her to be banished from the synagogue.

The law of Moses, in Leviticus 15:25–30, stated that a woman who had a discharge of blood for a prolonged period of time was unclean. Her bed was regarded as unclean. Even the furniture on which she sat was, under the law, regarded as unclean. Anyone who touched her bed, or her chair, or her clothes, was also unclean.

Obviously, a woman with this complaint could not attend the synagogue because of the uncleanness she would inflict on others. The only way she could be re-admitted to the synagogue under the law was to be healed of her discharge and then to offer a burnt offering and a sin offering, and the priest would make atonement for her.

Everyone in Capernaum would know of her and her complaint. Anyone banished from the synagogue would be well known. Over the past twelve years she had consulted doctor after doctor, seeking a cure. Mark writes that she "had suffered much under many different physicians" and had spent all her money in attending these doctors. Not only had she found no cure for her complaint, but the bleeding was getting worse.

This poor woman. A social outcast, poverty stricken, in a most weakened and depleted state of health, having lost blood constantly for twelve years. She had heard of the healing power of Jesus, and decided to risk all in an attempt to be cured. She had heard of many he had healed, and she *knew* if she could see him, he would heal her, too.

She couldn't possibly talk to him in front of everyone about her problem, but if she could just touch the hem of his cloak, she felt certain that his power would heal her.

Her faith was strong. She knew that the law required the Jews to have a fringe of blue in the hem, or border, of their garments to remind them of the commandments of the Lord. If she could not talk to Jesus, to touch this holy part of his garment would surely be enough.

If we could have watched this woman in the moments before she touched Jesus' garment, we would have seen her pushing her way through the thronging and noisy crowd, forcing her way closer and closer to Jesus. This was no mean feat, for a woman who knew she was a social outcast, who was weak in strength because of anaemia and who no doubt was by now naturally timid. The crowd would shrink back from her, fearing that she would touch them and make them unclean.

At last she was next to Jesus. She bent down and touched the edge of his garment. *Immediately* there surged through her body the power of healing, and she knew at once that she was cured!

But horror of horrors, Jesus stopped and said, "Who touched me"? The woman, who had wanted so desperately to do this thing in secret, shrank back in embarrassment. But Jesus' eyes caught her eyes, and she knew as he looked into her eyes that she could hide nothing from him. Trembling, she fell down before him, and in front of all the people, and told him not only that it was she who had touched him, but why she had touched him, and that she had been healed the moment she touched him.

Jesus' words to this brave woman said to her, "Daughter, your faith has made you well; go in peace."

While all this was going on, Jairus grew more and more agitated and was beside himself with anxiety about his twelve year old daughter. Remember that Jairus was standing next to Jesus during this incident. He was taking Jesus to his house. As the ruler of the synagogue, he would be expected to walk with Jesus. So he could do nothing but stand by while Jesus stopped and talked with the woman who had touched him.

Apart from his anxiety about the delay, what were Jairus' thoughts about this woman as she talked with Jesus. His little daughter had been born about the time this woman had been banished from the synagogue. His daughter was twelve. The woman's problem with her issue of blood had begun twelve years ago.

For twelve years, Jairus had loved his daughter and revelled in the joy of her childhood and growing up years. But through all these years, this woman had suffered more and more.

What had Jairus done for her, as ruler of the synagogue? Life had been comfortable for him, but not for her. All he had done was what the law said he should do. He had banished her from the synagogue and proclaimed her unclean.

Over the intervening years, she had suffered enormously under many doctors. She had no money left. Although the law said she was unclean, should Jairus, as ruler of the synagogue, have been more helpful to her over those years, and supported her, financially and spiritually, when there was no-one else to turn to?

But he had not. He had accepted the joy given to him by the hand of God in giving him a daughter twelve years ago, but he had neglected this poor woman. He had fulfilled the law to the letter, but he had shown no compassion or kindness or thoughtfulness to this woman.

And now, what was this Jesus saying to her? "Go in peace, your faith has made you well." He was not saying what the law said he should say — "Go to the priest and offer sacrifice, and he will make atonement for you." No, Jesus had healed her and sent her away in peace. He had given her all that Jairus and the law had not given her.

Three times now, Jesus had shown Jairus that mere observance of the ritualism of law was not the way of God. What was missing was compassion, based on a love of God and a reflection of His characteristics. First, there had been the healing of the man with the unclean spirit, second, the healing of the man with the withered hand (both on a Sabbath day), and third, the healing of this woman. Furthermore, Jesus had declared that she was no longer unclean because — not of the work of a Levitical priest — but because of her faith.

But Jesus had not yet finished with Jairus. As Jairus stood there beside Jesus, in utter desperation and turmoil of mind because of his daughter and this woman, a man from his house pushed his way through the crowd to where Jairus stood and said, "Your daughter is dead. Do not trouble the teacher any more."

The worst fears of Jairus were realised. It was too late. The delay had caused his daughter's death. Perhaps he buried his face in his hands at this terrible news. Perhaps he simply stood, numb with shock and grief. We are not told. What we are told is that Jesus heard the message given to Jairus and said, "Do not fear; only believe, and she shall be well."

So Jairus, in a mixture of heart-breaking grief and perplexity and utter bewilderment, led Jesus to his house. He took him to the room where his daughter lay, dead. We can only imagine Jairus' thoughts as he saw his little girl dead on the bed.

In the room were Jesus, Peter, James and John, Jairus and his wife. Under the law, to touch a dead body was to become unclean. Yet Luke writes that Jesus took the dead girl's hand and said, "Child, arise."

He didn't have to hold her hand. He could have merely commanded her to rise, as he did with Lazarus. I suggest there were two reasons why he took her by the hand. Jesus, with his infinite understanding of people, would realise that when the little girl awoke, she would see four strange men in her room with her parents. It would be of comfort to her if he held her hand. To have no physical contact with her would be frightening for her. He told her parents, "Give her something to eat."

The second reason was to show Jairus that compassion and love were paramount, and that he, Jesus, taught something greater than the law.

Jesus thus taught Jairus three powerful lessons, each one characterised by the love of God, through His Son, and by the healing power of God's spirit. In these three lessons, Jairus had gradually become more personally involved.

First, there were the two men in his synagogue, healed by Jesus on the Sabbath.

Second, the woman with the issue of blood, banished from the synagogue, perhaps, by Jairus himself. Certainly, he had neglected to care and support her for twelve years. The delay caused by her had resulted in his daughter's death.

Third, Jairus had seen his daughter brought back to life, with actions by Jesus which were not based on the law, but on love and kindness.

Surely, the healing hand of Jesus touched the heart of Jairus more closely, as each of these events unfolded — each one involving him more personally.

Each Sunday, we gather to remember Jesus in the emblems of bread and wine. When we do so, we recall that we, too, have responded to his call, also issued from Capernaum — "Come unto me, all you that labour, and I will give you rest."

"Come and stand here", said Jesus to the man with the withered hand. We come to him to stand before him with our withered hands, with our blindness, our deafness, our lameness — with our sinfulness. He has placed his hand on ours and made us whole in the forgiveness of our sins.

When we take the bread and wine, we recall the life that flowed out of him as he hung on the cross and died. He died because we have touched him with our sins. Just as he felt power leave him when the woman of faith touched the hem of his garment, so the power of life left him because of our touch, our sins.

The little daughter of Jairus, raised from death holding Jesus' hand as she awoke, reminds us that it will be his hand which lifts us from the death of mortality, to life and joy. "Give her something to eat", will be a far off echo as those raised to immortality sit down with him to eat the marriage supper of the Lamb.

God's love, manifested in Jesus, fills us with an awe which pervades every fibre of our being, and, as with Jairus, demands a response which comes from hearts softened by the healing hand of the Great Physician. In the words of Henry Twell's lovely hymn:

> "O Saviour Christ, thou too art man,
> Thou hast been troubled, tempted, tried,
> Thy kind but searching glance can scan
> The very wounds that shame would hide.
> Thy touch has still its ancient power;
> No word from thee can fruitless fall;
> Hear, in this solemn evening hour,
> And in thy mercy, heal us all."

9

On the mount of transfiguration

"After six days, Jesus took with him Peter and James and John his brother, and led them up a high mountain apart." (Matthew 17:1)

Peter, James and John formed a special group amongst Jesus' disciples. In times of stress, or on special occasions, he would leave the disciples, but take with him Peter, James and John.

On the occasion when he entered the house of Jairus to raise his twelve year old daughter from death, it was Peter, James and John he took with him. On the night of his most personal struggle, in the Garden of Gethsemane, he took Peter, James and John with him.

In one of the most dramatic events of Jesus' life, it was Peter, James and John who witnessed it. This was the occasion of the transfiguration of Jesus. Some Bible commentators are of the opinion that the mountain was in the vicinity of Mt. Herman, perhaps Mt. Herman itself, that mighty monarch of Israel which gazes majestically out over the land from its northern position near Caesarea Phillipi. What matters is not which mountain it was, but what took place there.

Jesus was transfigured before the three disciples. It is difficult for us to grasp the majesty and awe of this. The face of Jesus shone like the sun, and his clothes became as white as light. Mark describes his clothes as "glistening, intensely white", while Luke says that his clothes were "dazzling white", and that "the appearance of his countenance was altered."

To the astonished Peter, James and John, this would be shattering and mind-boggling. But this wasn't all! As the stunned three gazed at their Master, probably shading their eyes from the brilliance of his dazzling appearance, they saw an even more unexpected sight. Two other men were with Jesus, talking to him. Astoundingly, they recognised Moses … and Elijah!

Peter, always precipitous and overcome with the awe of the moment, blurted out, "Master, it is well that we are here. Let us make three booths, one for you, and one for Moses and one for Elijah", hardly knowing what he said.

Even as he spoke, a cloud overshadowed them, increasing the fear of the three disciples as it enveloped them in its mistiness. Out of the cloud came a sound like thunder. It was the voice of God Himself, saying, **"This is my beloved Son, in whom I am well pleased; hear ye him."**

This staggering event is one of the most significant events in all scripture. For Jesus, Moses and Elijah (also glorified) to talk together about "his departure which he was to accomplish at Jerusalem" (Luke 9:31) was unprecedented, both in the past and up to this present day. What this meant to the Lord can only be guessed at, but the whole event must have been tremendously strengthening to him as he contemplated what lay ahead.

Moses and Elijah represented the law and the prophets. Moses, the man whom God gave His law for the Jews to live by for the next fifteen hundred years. If the law could be represented by any man, that man was Moses.

Elijah the Tishbite, prophet of God three times over. First, when he appeared to King Ahab with his devastating message to return to the Lord God. Second, when he came in the form of John the Baptist, again with the same message, "Repent and return to God". The third occasion is still future. We know that Elijah, or someone in the spirit of Elijah, will appear again to the Jews of the last days. He will bring to them the same message — "Repent, and return to the Lord your God."

As Malachi wrote:

> "Behold, I will send you Elijah the prophet before the great and terrible day of the Lord comes. And he will turn the hearts of the fathers to the children, and the hearts of the children to their fathers." (Malachi 4:5–6)

We can see what tremendous significance there was in having the law and the prophets represented on the mountain with the Lord Jesus Christ. In this event, God chose to glorify all His dealings with men and women. He glorified the law and the prophets and His anointed Son, together, thus linking the past, present and future together all at once, depicting His whole plan and purpose with mankind, and glorifying it as a composite whole — a one-ness.

There is even more significance in the choosing of Moses and Elijah to appear with Jesus on the mountain. The circumstances of all three men were strongly linked together.

Moses, for example, like the Lord Jesus Christ, was a great deliverer. He was the means by which a great people were delivered from the slavery and fleshpots of Egypt to the Promised Land. But before he was considered ready for this task, he had to be prepared for it, and to develop a close relationship with God in the wilderness of Midian. For forty years, Moses lived in the wilderness as part of his preparation for his great task of deliverance.

For forty days and nights, Jesus was obedient to his Father in the wilderness and overcame the temptations which confronted him. As Moses was a mediator between the Children of Israel and God, as he pleaded for them despite their constant rebellion, haughtiness and sin, so do we have that greater mediator in the Lord Jesus Christ who pleads for us, in our faithlessness, our wavering, our disloyalty to our Master, in our sinfulness. As John Stainer wrote in one of his hymns:

> "Lord I have left thee, I have denied,
> Followed the world in my selfish pride;
> Lord, I have joined in the hateful cry,
> 'Slay him, away with him, crucify!'
> Lord, I have done it, oh! Ask me not how,
> Woven the thorns for thy tortured brow;
> Yet in his pity, so boundless and free,
> Jesus, the crucified, pleads for me."

Yes, there were strong links between Moses and Jesus, links which brought them together on the mountain. In both cases, the call came strongly, "Return, return to the ways of the Lord God Almighty." Deliverance is not merely deliverance from a place or from a set of physical circumstances. It is deliverance from ourselves. Just as the needle of a compass swings unerringly towards the north, so do our natures swing unerringly towards sin, the ways of the flesh, and away from the ways of the spirit.

And Elijah. Elijah was not a deliverer in the sense that Moses was and Jesus is. But, like them, his dominating message was, and will be, *"Return."*

This call to return to God cries out from all of scripture. From the time of Adam's sin, the plea from God to man is "Return to Me." We find it at the time of the flood, when God found people who were prepared to be faithful to Him and start again to fill the earth with people.

But those people, like all before them, swung away from God's ways. Right through the history of the Jews we find the call again and again. Isaiah cried, "Thus saith the Lord, 'I have swept away your transgressions like a cloud, and your sins like mist; return to Me, for I have redeemed you'." And again, "Let him return to the Lord that He may have mercy on him."

Jeremiah takes up the call in God's words, " 'If you return, O Israel', says the Lord, 'to Me you should return.' "

And Malachi, "From the days of your fathers you have turned aside from My statutes and have not kept them. Return to Me, and I will redeem you, says the Lord of hosts."

This, then, was the message of Elijah the prophet. A remarkable man. His beginnings are unknown and he did not see death. He leaps into the pages of scripture unannounced as Elijah the Tishbite, with the stunning message to King Ahab, "As the Lord the God of Israel lives, before whom I stand, there shall be neither dew nor rain these years, except by my word." Having delivered this short, crisp message, Elijah disappears. He came, and just as suddenly, he is gone.

His message to Ahab and Israel was, "Return to the Lord."

Elijah, in the form of John the Baptist, appeared again eight hundred years later, when he came with the same message, but also to announce Jesus as the Messiah. Jesus acknowledged him and his work by saying, "There has risen no greater than John the Baptist ... If you are willing to accept it, he is Elijah who is to come."

When Elijah confronted Ahab, he was sudden, direct and uncompromising in his message to him. John the Baptist was ruthless in the delivery of **his** message of repentance, "You brood of vipers! Who warned you to flee from the wrath to come? Bear fruits that befit repentance ... "

When he appears again, to the Jews, to "turn the hearts of the fathers to the children, and the hearts of the children to their fathers", we can expect that his message to the Jews will be just as hard-hitting, just as non-compromising.

Yes, Elijah had strong links with Moses and Jesus. Not as a deliverer, but as a man who brought people back to God, and as a man who introduced the Jews to Jesus in the past and will do so again in the future.

Why do we need to return to the Lord? Surely we have never left him? We are not as the Jews of Old Testament times who rejected God to worship other gods.

Quite true, but it is important to examine ourselves from time to time to ensure we are not little by little drifting away from the ways of God in our lives. Paul wrote to the Colossian ecclesia:

> "Continue in the faith, stable and steadfast, not shifting from the hope of the gospel which you have heard ... " (Colossians 1:23)

We cannot ignore the fact that amongst the true followers of God today, there is evidence that the ways of the world have drifted in among us. Apathy towards the Word of God, broken marriages, divorce, child abuse, drug addiction, alcohol abuse — all reflective of the ways of the flesh and not the ways of the spirit, have infiltrated the ranks of God's followers. We may not bow down to false gods of wood and stone, as the Children of Israel did, but in other ways, our hearts have drifted from God's ways to the ways of the flesh, just as theirs did. The needle of our compasses needs to be looked at often to make sure they are pointed in the right direction.

As we return to the mount of transfiguration, we like Peter, James and John, gaze at Jesus, Moses and Elijah as they discuss the departure of Jesus from Jerusalem. Ahead, lies his crucifixion and death. But beyond that terrible experience is his mighty resurrection. Forty days later, in the presence of his disciples, he ascends to heaven in a cloud to be with his Father.

> "This Jesus, who was taken up from you into heaven, will come in the same way as you saw him go into heaven", angels told the apostles. (Acts 1:11)

The dazzling glory which shone with the brightness of lightning from Jesus on the mount of transfiguration, will shine from him again when he comes again in his descent from heaven in "power and great glory". On that day, the dawn of a new era heralding the Kingdom of God on earth, people all over the world will look into the sky to see the brilliance of God's glory, and the brilliance of His glorified Son, as he descends to earth accompanied by myriads of angels and the reverberating sound of a mighty trumpet call.

Then will occur the great resurrection of all those who have died in Christ, and the gathering of them, and those who are alive at his coming, into the air to meet him, as he comes to earth as King of kings and Lord of lords.

Amongst the millions of faithful followers down through the ages to welcome him will be those who witnessed his glory on the mount of transfiguration — Moses, Elijah, Peter, James and John. Once more, they will see his glistening glory as they saw it on the mount. But this time, it will not be his departure they will discuss, but his Kingship as he prepares to occupy the ancient throne of David in Jerusalem.

Then, the whole world will see his dazzling glory, and the earth will be filled with the knowledge of the glory of God Himself.

Amen, come Lord Jesus.

10

Two days at the temple

It is about six months before the crucifixion. On this particular day, we find Jesus in the Temple at Jerusalem, for he is attending the Feast of Tabernacles. Over the next two days, he will show the people he is the Saviour of the world.

Israel's Summer is almost over and Autumn is approaching. The events we will consider take place at the end of the Feast of Tabernacles, or just after.

The feast of Tabernacles took place in the seventh month (our October). It lasted eight days. Jesus didn't arrive at the feast until the fourth day. But it is what he said on the last day of the feast which is of particular interest. Here is what he said (John 7:37–38):

> "On the last day of the feast, Jesus stood up and proclaimed, 'If anyone thirst, let him come to me and drink. He who believes in me, as the scripture has said, "Out of his heart shall flow rivers of living water." ' "

This was a spectacular appeal to the people.

Why did Jesus choose to proclaim himself in this way at the end of the Feast of Tabernacles? Let's think about the background to this important annual feast in Jewish life.

We find God's instructions about this feast in Exodus, Leviticus and Numbers. People were to dwell in booths (tents) during the eight days of the feast to remind them of the forty year journey through the wilderness. Specific animal sacrifices were to be made on each of the eight days.

In later years, other customs were introduced by the Jews. One was that on each day (except the Sabbath) a priest went down to the Pool of Siloam and drew a golden pitcher of water, which was carried back to the Temple and poured into a silver basin. But on the eighth day (called the great day of the feast) this ritual was not carried out.

The Feast of Tabernacles began on a Friday and ended the following Friday — thus involving eight days. The second day of the feast was a Sabbath, and the last day, the eighth, the great day, was the day before the next Sabbath. **It is important to note that on the eighth day, the priest did not go down to the Pool of Siloam to draw water, as he did on all of the other days.**

It was on the eighth day, the great day (John 7:37) that Jesus stood up and proclaimed,

"If any one thirst, let him come to me and drink."

Here was one of the great invitations of Jesus to the people. Another was at Capernaum, earlier in his ministry, when he cried, "Come unto me, all you who labour and are heavy laden, and I will give you rest."

It was the custom of Jesus to sit down as he taught the people at the Temple, but now he stood up so that all could see him, so important was this invitation. The word "proclaimed", in its Greek meaning, means to "cry out" or to "call aloud". Jesus stood up, and cried out in a loud voice, **"If any one thirst, let him come to me and drink."**

Here, at the Temple, on this last day of the feast, Jesus compares himself and his invitation with the ritual of the law. The souls and hearts of the people were dried up and parched. In their need, their thirst would never be quenched by the law. "If any one thirst, let him come to *me* and drink", was, and is, the invitation of Jesus.

Jesus fed the crowds with bread, representing himself as the Bread of Life, on the shore of the Sea of Galilee, on at least two occasions. Matthew tells us that "when he saw the crowds, he had compassion on them."

Now at the Temple, he invites them to come to him and drink. Again, he has compassion on the people because he again sees them as sheep not having a shepherd. All week, they have been caught up with the priests' daily ritual of bringing water from the Pool of Siloam — water brought by the priests who were neglecting the spiritual needs of their people. Paraphrasing Jesus' words, he cries "Come to me! The water from Siloam is not the living water. I am the living water. He who thirsts, come to me and drink."

We will return to the Pool of Siloam shortly.

The day draws to a close, and Jesus goes to spend the night on the Mount of Olives, no doubt at the home of Mary, Martha and Lazarus, at Bethany.

It is now the next day, the Sabbath. It is early in the morning. Jesus is again at the Temple, and the crowds are there waiting for him. His words of the previous day had warmed their hearts. "All the people came to him, and he sat down and taught them." (John 8:2).

As he speaks to them, there is a stir and a bustle on the outside of the crowd. Heads turn to see some scribes and Pharisees pushing a woman in front of them through the crowd. They pushed her roughly to where Jesus was sitting and said to him, "Teacher, this woman has been caught in the act of adultery."

We can imagine the electric response these words would have on the crowds around Jesus. What would he do? What would he say? "In the law", said the woman's accusers, "Moses commanded us to stone such. What do you say about her?"

The woman had clearly sinned, and so had the man who was with her. Strangely, there is no mention of the man. Under the law, the penalty for adultery was death. (Leviticus 20:10). The law also contained a principle that accusations about various acts of sin had to be made by two or three witnesses. The charge could not be upheld by one witness alone. (Deuteronomy 17:6). The law also stated that the witnesses were to be the first to cast the stones aimed at killing the sinner.

We see these principles reflected in the way Jesus dealt with this case. Jesus' first response to the question by the scribes and Pharisees was to bend down and write on the ground. He then stood up and said to them, "Let him who is without sin among you be the first to throw a stone at her." This was a correct application of the law, with one important exception. Jesus linked their accusation with their own sin. It took them all by surprise. They all, one by one, stole away.

Jesus looked at the woman and asked,

"Woman, where are they? Has no-one condemned you?"

"No one, Lord."

"Neither do I condemn you; go and do not sin again."

The Pharisees were furious on two counts. First, the woman had not been stoned as they believed she should have been under the law. Second, Jesus had ignored the law stating that two or three witnesses must prove a case. He, and he alone, had decided the woman should be forgiven and set free.

Jesus had done what the Pharisees had not done. He had brought together the *two* elements of the God's law, not just one. It was true that God had stipulated in the law that the penalty for adultery was death. But He had also said that all judgement must be tempered with compassion.

It was not as if the Pharisees didn't know about God's requirement for compassion. There are at least sixty references to it in the Old Testament. Here is just one example from the words of Micah's prophecy:

> "What does the Lord require of you? To act justly, and to love mercy, and to walk humbly with your God." (Micah 6:8)

Jesus, in his response to the Pharisees reminded them of their own relationship to God. "Let him who is *without sin* cast the first stone." In effect, Jesus said to the Pharisees, "Think about your own relationship to the Father. Are you, in your own sin, acceptable to Him? Deal with that before you condemn this woman for her sin."

The lesson is clear for all of us. Before we accuse, condemn or even criticise someone, first consider our own position before God. Our own sinfulness. We may have a log in our eye, whereas our brother or sister may have only a speck in theirs.

Jesus had shown compassion. "Neither do I condemn you." But he adds, "Go, and do not sin again."

Jesus is greater than the law. He had shown that the day before — "If anyone thirst, let him come to me and drink." Now, he forgives this woman, admonishes her, and sets her free.

In his continuing discussion with the Pharisees following this incident, we see him repeat this great principle of freedom again and again:

John 8:31 "If you continue in my word, you are truly my disciples, and you will know the truth, and the truth will make you free."

8:34–36 "Everyone who commits sin is a slave to sin. The slave does not continue in the house forever; the son continues for ever. So, if the Son makes you free, you will be free indeed."

It is still the Sabbath, and the events of this day were not over yet. The infuriated and frustrated Pharisees took up stones to throw at Jesus, but "he hid himself and went out of the Temple."

John continues his fascinating account of this Sabbath day by telling us that "as he (Jesus) passed by, he saw a man blind from his birth." (John 9:1) Responding to a question by his disciples about this man, he told them the he was the light of the world. Here was a blind man, for whom there had never been light. Jesus reminds his disciples that he is the light of the world.

This was the second time this day he had said this. He had told the Pharisees the same thing. "I am the light of the world; he who follows me will not walk in darkness, but will have the light of life." (John 8:12).

Here is this man, born blind, a beggar. All his life, he had known only darkness. He had never seen anything. He didn't know what people looked like, or trees or buildings or roads or the sky. He had never seen the sun or the moon. He had never seen the food he ate. Darkness. And Jesus said, "I am the light of the world." The man had never seen light, but Jesus said, "I am the light."

Jesus did two things to test the faith of this blind man. First, he spat on the ground and made clay and rubbed it in the man's eyes. Second, he told him to go and wash in the Pool of Siloam.

Rubbing wet clay in someone's eyes would certainly not help him to see. It would make the problem worse. Remember, this took place in the Temple. The Pool of Siloam was at the other end of the city, through crowded streets filled with people who were still there from the Feast of Tabernacles. To reach the pool, the man had to make his way across the city, and down steep steps to the pool. This was quite a challenge to the blind man.

We can see him as he feels his way through the crowds, his eyes full of moist clay, groping and fumbling his way along, bumping into impatient people. We see him feeling his way down the steep steps, down, down to the Pool of Siloam, deep below the level of the city streets.

This was the pool from which the priests had drawn water for the Feast of Tabernacles each day over the past week. The meaning of this had been symbolic.

Siloam was much in the people's minds that week. All week, they had seen the priests draw water from the pool and carry it to the Temple. Some of the people would accompany the priest. Now, Jesus has told the blind man to go to this very pool and wash his eyes there. Jesus was reinforcing his message to the people that he was the living water, and his healing power was effective and real, not symbolic. Siloam without Jesus was nothing. Siloam with Jesus was everything. The law without Jesus was ineffective of itself. The law with Jesus was complete.

Now, as the blind man reached the water, and splashed water up into his eyes, he could suddenly see for the first time in his life.

Characteristically, the scriptural record of this mighty event is an understatement:

> "So he went and washed and came back seeing." (John 9:7)

But the man was *changed!* His whole face was lit up with a new light borne of wonder and awe at all he saw. No wonder his acquaintances hardly recognised him!

But the Pharisees were angry. It was the Sabbath. They asked the man how he had received his sight. They called his parents and asked them. They called the man back a second time and said, "Give God the praise; we know this man is a sinner". Finally, they cast him out of the Temple.

One wonders whether these Pharisees knew that they were fulfilling a prophecy made by Isaiah seven hundred years earlier — words which are chillingly similar to those used by the Pharisees:

> "Hear the word of the Lord, you who tremble at His Word. 'Your brethren
> who hate you and cast you out for My name's sake have said, "Let the

Lord be glorified, that we may see your joy", but it is they who shall be put to shame.' " (Isaiah 66:5)

So the man was cast out of the Temple because he confessed that Jesus was from God, "If this man were not from God, he could do nothing."

The story does not end there. Jesus "heard that they had cast him out, and having found him, he said, 'Do you believe in the son of man?' " The compassion and understanding of Jesus is limitless. This man would be devastated and confused. He had just been given the greatest gift of his life, and his religious leaders had cast him out of the Temple and made him a social outcast. We can imagine his feelings of confusion, bewilderment and loss, all tangled up in the midst of his joy at receiving his sight.

Jesus knew how he would feel. He looked for him. He found him. Furthermore, he did it openly in front of the Pharisees (John 9:40).

In the cases of both the woman taken in adultery, and the man born blind, we see the effect of the compassion of Jesus, in contrast with the harshness of the attitude of the Pharisees.

In both cases, the reaction of the Pharisees was, "Get rid of these people. Get rid of the woman! Stone her to death. She is a sinner"

"Get rid of this man! Cast him out! He has proclaimed Jesus as the Son of God."

It's the easy way out. "Get rid of these troublesome people and let's get on with our lives." But the way of Jesus is different. "Consider your own sin first", he told the Pharisees, "Consider your own relationship with God before you condemn others."

Jesus took the trouble to search among the crowded Temple for the man he had healed of his blindness. He searched until he found the man who had been thrown out of the Temple. His words to him in front of everyone were, "Don't be afraid, you have found a greater Temple, for you have the light of the world. You have found the Son of God. It is he who is speaking to you."

Over these two days at the Temple, we have a picture of the role of Jesus as the Saviour of the world:

- He *invites* the people to come to him, as the water of life.

- He *forgives* a sinner and grants her freedom.
- He *heals* a man born blind, and shows great kindness to him after the Pharisees had thrown him out of the Temple.

Invitation — Forgiveness — Healing.

This is the process for all who choose to come to him, seeking forgiveness and healing. He says to us, as he said to those involved over those two days:

"If anyone thirsts, let him come to me and drink." *His invitation*

"Neither do I condemn you. Go, and do not sin again." *His forgiveness*

"Go, wash in the Pool of Siloam and receive your sight." *His healing*

In this picture, we see the compassion of Jesus at work. His whole ministry reflected his compassion. He healed the sick, gave sight to the blind and hearing to the deaf, healed people who could not walk, fed the people, cuddled children in his arms, forgave people their sins, restored to life the daughter of Jairus, the young man from Nain and Lazarus.

Perhaps the greatest act of Jesus' compassion is seen as he hung on the cross. Here we find a depth of feeling and compassion which shone through the darkness and cruelty of whipping, pain, rejection and sorrow. Jesus spoke those words of compassion and forgiveness which only he could have spoken:

"Father, forgive them, for they know not what they do."

As we stand at the foot of the cross each week, "in remembrance of him", we, too, must seek forgiveness for the things we have done, for the many times we have neglected to show compassion.

We look to Jesus, who provides us with the living water of eternal life; who is the light of life; who has forgiven us our sins; who has opened our eyes in new sight. It is Jesus who has found us amongst the crowds and has taken us to himself.

11

The meal at Bethany

We find Jesus with his disciples at Bethany, at the house of Simon the leper, and his children, Mary, Martha and Lazarus.

Jesus has come to Jerusalem on his last visit before his crucifixion. He is only days away from the event he was undoubtedly dreading. He knows full well what lies ahead. His knowledge of the scriptures provides him with every terrible detail of what he must expect.

He knows.

> *Psalm 22:* "I am poured out like water, and all my bones are out of joint; my heart is like wax, it is melted within my breast ... my tongue cleaves to my jaws ... "
>
> They have pierced my hands and feet ... I can count all my bones — they stare and gloat over me."
>
> *Isaiah 53:* "He was despised and rejected by men ... he was despised and we esteemed him not.
>
> He was wounded for our transgressions, and bruised for our iniquities. By his stripes (from Roman scourging), we are healed"
>
> *Isaiah 50:* "He did not hide his face from shame and spitting. They plucked out the hair from his cheeks ... "
>
> *Isaiah 52:* "His appearance was so marred, beyond human semblance ... "

Oh, yes, he knows what awaits him, only days away. His agonised prayer to his Father in the Garden of Gethsemane a few days later gives us an indication of how he felt about the dreadful hours ahead. Little wonder he cried out to his Father, *"If it be possible, remove this cup from me."*

His visit to Bethany is only four days before these dreadful events. He has come to the home of the little family he loves.

It is the time of the evening meal. As is the custom, they recline on pallets around the low table, its surface about six inches from the floor. Those present are Simon, Lazarus, Martha, Mary, Jesus and the disciples — seventeen in all. John adds the homely comment that Martha served.

It is a remarkable meal in a sense, this meal at Bethany. Never before had a man who had been dead for four days been brought back to life again. And now here he is, at this meal, and as if to emphasise the point, John writes (John 12:1), "Jesus came to Bethany where Lazarus was". And in the next verse, "Lazarus was one of those at table with him".

The remarkableness of Lazarus' presence has not escaped the Jews either, for in chapter 12:9, John goes on to say that a great crowd of Jews came to the house, not only to see Jesus, but "also to see Lazarus, whom (Jesus) had raised from the dead" only four months earlier.

Many of the crowd here tonight were at Bethany four months earlier when this amazing resurrection took place. They remembered that a messenger had arrived with the news that Jesus was coming. But Lazarus had died four days earlier, and was well and truly laid in a tomb. Jesus was too late. Four days too late.

The Jews here remembered that Mary and Martha had sent urgently for Jesus when Lazarus was critically ill. But Jesus had not come immediately. While he delayed, Lazarus died. His sisters and his father were grief-stricken. Had their beloved master let them down?

Four days later came the message that Jesus was coming! Someone went to tell Martha, and she left the house and went to meet him. She came to him before he had entered Bethany and said, "Lord, if you had been here, my brother would not have died".

Is there a touch of rebuke of Jesus here? "Lord, you should have come when we asked you to. Had you come, Lazarus would still be alive". She knew Jesus could have healed Lazarus. It had never occurred to her that Jesus could also raise him from death.

Martha ran back to the house to tell Mary that Jesus had arrived, although he had not yet entered the village. He made no attempt to go to Mary, but waited for Mary to come to him.

Mary came to Jesus with tears running down her cheeks. She sobbed the same words as Martha had spoken, "Lord, if you had been here my brother would not have died".

Jesus was a man of great compassion. It moved him deeply to see Mary so upset. He knew why he had delayed his arrival, but she didn't. To Mary, and to Martha, Lazarus had died because Jesus hadn't come when they asked him to.

"When Jesus saw her weeping, and the Jews who came with her also weeping, he was deeply moved in spirit, and troubled", and he wept, no doubt at the sight of Mary's grief.

It is as well for us to pause here a moment, to reflect upon the fact that our own prayerful requests are not always answered immediately. It is not always God's way to remove obstacles and problems from us. There is often a purpose behind leaving us with our trials and problems — a purpose not always perceived by us at the time — just as Mary and Martha did not perceive the reason for Jesus' delay in responding to their request.

We are not alone in this. There is plenty of scriptural precedent in which God chooses to leave someone in their predicament to test their faith. But *always* He provides us with the strength to cope with our trials if we trust in Him.

Take Joseph, for example, when at seventeen years of age he was sold into Egypt, alone and far from his family. Then, worse still, he is thrown into prison for something he didn't do! If ever a man could have felt rejected and ignored, it was Joseph. But his faith in God was strong, and God blessed him.

David is another example, hunted for years by Saul. Imploring God to deliver him, to take him away from his misery, to destroy his enemies. But God chose not to deliver him immediately from these trials.

In the same way, lack of an obvious response to our own prayers does not mean that God is ignoring us. He is helping us to cope, and testing our faith in Him. He is building up our reliance on His strength. He has told us, "I will never leave you or forsake you". He never left Joseph or David or many others who cried out for deliverance from their difficulties. The time came when He delivered them.

So Jesus stood in front of the tomb of Lazarus with Mary and Martha. He said, **"Take away the stone"**

It is not hard to imagine the almost audible gasp from the crowd as Jesus gave this command. What was Jesus doing? They saw him pray quietly as a ripple of tension spread through the crowd. There was now utter silence. The atmosphere must have been electric. What was Jesus doing? There stood the open tomb, the stone rolled away, the crowd staring in incredulous awe. Suddenly the silence was shattered by Jesus crying out, **"Lazarus, come forth!"**

If there had been an audible gasp from the crowd when the stone was rolled away, the crowd must have caught their breath and fallen backwards with a cry, when, from out from the darkness of the tomb emerged Lazarus, grotesque in the cloths which bound his hands and feet and face. **"Untie him and let him go"**, commanded Jesus.

Now, four months after that dramatic event, as Lazarus reclines at the table with Jesus at Bethany, this mighty happening is imprinted on all their minds. It is also on the minds of the Jews who are clamouring outside for a glimpse of Jesus and Lazarus.

As we watch, there occurs that lovely event which meant so much to Jesus. With his horrible suffering and death only four days away, his heart goes out to Mary as she produces an alabaster flask containing about a pound weight of the most expensive and costly ointment. It is pure nard, estimated to cost around $9,000 today.

In loving adoration, she breaks the flask and anoints his feet. (Matthew and Mark record that she anointed his head, so it is possible she poured it over both his head and feet).

It is an act of the greatest love, and Jesus, we can be sure, is much moved and touched by Mary's love in doing this for him. His had been a life of suffering, and much greater suffering lies just ahead. How beautiful is this devotion of Mary's to Jesus.

As we watch, the atmosphere is suddenly chilled by Judas saying, "Why this waste? The ointment should have been sold and the money given to the poor".

This is an absolute insult to Jesus. In effect, Judas is saying, "Don't waste that stuff on Jesus. Give the money to those who need it". Worse still, that is not the real motive of Judas. His real motive, John records, was because Judas was a thief and wanted the money for himself.

How must Jesus be feeling about this? Surely he must feel very hurt at these words of Judas, especially as they are in stark contrast to the love Mary has just shown. "Let her alone", is Jesus' response to Judas. "For she has done a beautiful thing to me. You will always have the poor with you, but you will not always have me ... Truly I say to you, wherever this gospel is preached in the whole world, what she has done will be told in memory of her".

So Jesus rebukes Judas, and it seems that that rebuke was the catalyst which causes Judas to go to the Chief Priest and offer to deliver Jesus to them for thirty pieces of silver. "From that moment onward, he sought an opportunity to betray him".

It is worth contrasting Judas' response to the rebuke of Jesus with David's response to Nathan, when Nathan rebuked him for taking Bathsheba and killing Uriah. David's reaction was immediate repentance: "I have sinned against the Lord". Judas' reaction was not repentance, but a determination to deliver Jesus into the hands of his enemies.

There is therefore a stark contrast in attitude between David and Judas. Even so, Jesus did not reject Judas, for Judas was still amongst the disciples in the upper room. He partook of the bread of the last supper.

Incredibly, at that last supper, the disciples argued amongst themselves about who was the greatest. Jesus rose from the table and washed their feet, including the feet of Judas. But the treachery of Judas was very much in Jesus' mind, for he said, "You are not all clean. He who ate my bread has lifted his heel against me". In these words, we are reminded not only of Judas, but also of Ahithophel, the grandfather of Bathsheba, who, years later, deserted David to go to Absalom, because of the great wrong David had committed against his granddaughter.

As David recorded of Ahithophel in Psalm 55:12–13 — words which could equally apply to Judas,

> "It is not an enemy who taunts me — then I could bear it … but it is you, my equal, my companion, my familiar friend …
>
> His speech was smoother that butter, yet war was in his heart; his words were softer than oil, yet they were drawn swords".

Both Judas and Ahithophel rejected the way of God, and both committed suicide.

The meal at Bethany is full of contrasts:

- Jesus was warmed and touched by Mary's loving devotion … but deeply hurt by Judas' lack of feeling for him.
- The flask of precious ointment is contrasted with Judas' moneybox.
- Judas received thirty pieces of silver, but Mary's ointment was worth more than 300 pence.
- Judas was a thief and covetous; Mary gave all she had for Jesus.
- Judas ended his life in suicide and is remembered as a betrayer. Mary's love for Jesus shines down through the centuries, and she will be lifted by his hand to join him in the Kingdom.[1]

What comfort Mary's love must have been to Jesus over the next few days. He would remember it in the face of hatred and revenge against him; in the face of false testimony against him; in the ordeal of soldiers spitting at him, tearing at his beard, beating him up, tearing his clothes off him, yelling and jeering at him sarcastically.

He would remember Mary's devotion when the Roman whip lashed his back and shoulders and tore his flesh to shreds, and as his tortured and pulverised body jerked with agony as they belted the nails into his hands and feet.

In a sense, the table at Bethany was the table of their Lord. After his ascension, the family would gather around that same table at mealtimes and talk about him and remember how he reclined with them at that meal only a few days before his death. They would think of all he did and said, and rejoice above all that he was alive again.

---

[1] The thoughts of Harry Whittaker in his book *Studies in the Gospel*, P. 548 are acknowledged.

Let us in thought and spirit bring our figurative alabaster jars of ointment and anoint his head and his feet as our expression of love for him, as we remember him every day. Jesus came to Bethany to raise Lazarus from death. He is coming back to us to take his followers from the death of mortality.

Come, Lord Jesus!

12

The final week

It is Monday, and we are at Bethany. Bethany is a couple of miles from Jerusalem, but separated from it by the Mount of Olives.

We need to get this Monday into perspective. It is the beginning of the week in which Jesus is to be crucified. He was crucified on Friday, and we are at Bethany on the previous Monday.

This week is to be one of the most difficult for Jesus in the whole of his three and a half year ministry. He will come into a head-on confrontation with the Jewish leaders on the Wednesday, and on Thursday, late at night, he will fight his personal battle in the Garden of Gethsemane. "Father", he would pray, "if it be possible, let this cup pass from me".

Jesus is at Bethany on this Monday with his disciples. They had spent Sunday night there at the home of his close friends, Mary, Martha and Lazarus and their father, Simon, and as they set out from Bethany, it was probably early afternoon.

As we watch, we see a huge crowd coming up the path from Bethany as they climb up the slope of the Mount of Olives on the last leg of their journey to Jerusalem. In the midst of the crowd, we see Jesus, riding on a colt — an ass's colt. His disciples are with him, and there are dozens, probably hundreds, of people all around him — in front, to the sides and behind him — all jostling together as they all try to get onto this narrow path leading over the Mount of Olives leading from Bethany to Jerusalem.

Many of these people are those Jesus had healed. We know, for example, that the two blind men Jesus healed at Jericho on the previous day are there. Matthew tells us "they received their sight and followed him". (Matthew 20:34). There were many others whom Jesus had healed. Most were convinced he was the long awaited Messiah.

All roads leading into Jerusalem were packed with people because it was Passover week. People came from all over Israel to Jerusalem for Passover week each year. Husbands, wives, children, men travelling alone, old folk and young folk came in their thousands.

As Jesus came to the top of the Mount of Olives, he saw Jerusalem directly in front of him. He had walked this path many times before and was very familiar with this sudden revealing of Jerusalem as he reached the top of the Mount of Olives. But this visit was like no other. We can pick up some of the excitement here in Luke 19:37–40. Jesus has begun his descent towards Jerusalem, and the crowd suddenly erupted with joy and excitement as they escorted the man they were convinced was their Messiah, their King, on the downward slope of the Mount of Olives, with Jerusalem now in full view:

> "As he was now drawing near, at the descent of the Mount of Olives, the whole multitude of the disciples began to rejoice and praise God with a loud voice for all the mighty works that they had seen, saying, 'Blessed is the King who comes in the name of the Lord! Peace in heaven and glory in the highest!' " (Luke 19:37–38)

When Jesus saw Jerusalem, he wept. He said, "Would that even today you knew the things that make for peace! But now they are hid from your eyes ... "

The people thronging around Jesus and proclaiming him as their King were thinking of the mighty prophecy of Zechariah:

> "Rejoice greatly, O daughter of Zion! Shout aloud, O daughter of Jerusalem! Lo, your king comes to you; triumphant and victorious is he, humble and riding on an ass, on a colt, the foal of an ass". (Zechariah 9:9)

Jesus' entry into Jerusalem on this Monday of his crucifixion week was only a partial fulfilment of this prophecy. We note in the very next verse of Zechariah that "he shall command peace to the nations; his dominion shall be from sea to sea, and from the River to the ends of the earth".

This is still future, and it seems that at his second coming, Jesus will once again ride on a donkey into Jerusalem. But then, he will be recognised as King of kings, and Lord of lords by the whole world.

Crossing the brook Kedron, Jesus ascended the hill opposite the Mount of Olives and entered the Temple. Mark tells us "he looked around at everything (and) as it was already late, he went out to Bethany with the twelve".

Jesus was furious at what he saw in the Temple. Three and a half years ago, he had thrown the traders and money-changers out of the Temple. Now, they were at it again, selling their goods and sacrificial animals at exorbitant prices in Passover week to the thousands of people who swarmed in and out of the Temple. We can imagine Jesus' smouldering anger as he walked back over the Mount to Bethany that night.

Next morning, Tuesday, he walked across the Mount of Olives again, into Jerusalem and went straight to the Temple. Mark describes what happened:

> "He entered the temple and began to drive out those who sold and those who bought in the temple, and he overturned the tables of the money-changers and the seats of those who sold pigeons ... And he taught and said to them, 'Is it not written "My house shall be called a place of prayer for all the nations? But you have made it a den of robbers" ' ". (Mark 11:15–17)

We need to pause here to consider the effect on the Jewish leaders of this dramatic and unexpected happening as Jesus stormed into the temple and hurled the tables to the ground and scattered the money-changers' money across the floor of the temple. The Jewish religious leaders had been trying for weeks to trap Jesus and kill him. Only weeks before, he had raised Lazarus to life, and this had caused a huge number of people to flock to Jesus. This was the reason why they had accompanied him, singing his praises and proclaiming him King as he entered Jerusalem the day before on a donkey:

> "Jesus found a young ass and sat upon it; as it is written, 'Fear not, daughter of Zion; behold, your king is coming, sitting on an ass's colt ... the crowd that had been with him when he called Lazarus out of the tomb and raised him from the dead bore witness. The reason why the crowd went to meet him was that they heard he had done this sign". (John 12:14–15, 17–18)

In the previous three and a half years of his ministry, Jesus had deliberately avoided being trapped by these leaders. "My time has not yet come", he had said.

But now, he knew that in three days' time he would be arrested and then killed. It wasn't necessary to avoid these men any more. If we look carefully at his actions and words on this Tuesday and then Wednesday, we find him time and time again devastatingly denouncing these hypocritical and self-seeking leaders.

At the same time, the leaders stepped up their efforts to trap him. The day after Jesus overthrew those in the temple, the Jewish leaders confronted Jesus directly and challenged his authority, referring to the temple overthrow:

> "By what authority are you doing these things, or who gave you the authority to do them?" (Mark 11:28)

Jesus answered their question by asking whether the baptism of John the Baptist was from heaven or from men. This was a clever answer. They chose not to reply, saying only, "We cannot tell". "Neither do I tell you by what authority I do these things", replied Jesus.

The Jewish leaders didn't let up. That same day (Wednesday) they decided to challenge him by sending, first, some Pharisees to entrap him. "They were amazed at him", we are told. Second, some Sadducees were sent packing. Finally, a scribe was sent. The result of that challenge was, "After that, no one dared to ask him any question".

But Jesus was not finished with these self-righteous leaders. Up to now, he had answered *their* questions. Now, on this same occasion, he openly attacks them. Remember that they are still present, there among the crowd, so they heard his direct denunciation of them first hand. First, he tells the crowd and his disciples:

> "The scribes and the Pharisees sit on Moses' seat; so practice and observe whatever they tell you, but do not practice ...

Then he hurls at the Jewish leaders:

> ... Woe to you, scribes and Pharisees, hypocrites! You tithe mint and cumin and have neglected the weightier matters of the law — justice, mercy and faith.

> ... Woe to you, scribes and Pharisees, hypocrites! You are like white-washed tombs which appear outwardly beautiful, but within they are full of dead men's bones and all uncleanness.
>
> ... You serpents, you brood of vipers, how are you to escape being sentenced to hell?" (Matthew 23:23–33)

To hurl an accusation at the leaders of the people that, in today's language, they are a brood of snakes, outwardly acceptable, but filthy within, was the last straw for them. From that moment on, the die was cast. Humiliated before the people by this man they had grown to hate, they slunk away with murder in their hearts. This man represented a great threat to their authority, their power and their way of life. The people were calling him a king and referring to him as their long-awaited Messiah — Son of David — Christ, the anointed one. They simply *had* to find a way to get rid of him.

We can imagine them plotting their next move, late into Wednesday night. If they were to arrest him, it had to be at night when there were no people about, otherwise there would be a revolt. And they had to have him crucified by early the following morning, before the people were aware of what had happened.

On Wednesday afternoon, when the Jewish leaders were developing their plans on how to arrest Jesus, he and his disciples set off over the Mount of Olives to spend the night at Bethany. It would be Jesus' last night before his arrest.

On the way, they paused and sat down, somewhere on the Mount. There, the disciples asked him a question. They were puzzled about something he had said before they left Jerusalem to set out on their journey to Bethany. Now, about twenty minutes later (the time it took to walk from Jerusalem to the Mount of Olives) they asked him about it. In Jerusalem, he had said of Jerusalem,

> "You will not see me again, until you say, 'Blessed is he who comes in the name of the Lord' " (Matthew 23:39)

Thinking about this, the disciples asked him,

> "Tell us, when will this be, and what will be the sign of your coming and of the close of the age?" (Matthew 24:3)

Jesus told them what lay ahead for his followers. He told them that he would come again, this time in power and great glory. He told them that before he came again, there would be wars and rumours of wars, famines, earthquakes and nations fighting against each other.

He especially told them that there would be a time of great tribulation, greater than any tribulation before, in which his followers would suffer greatly, and even be killed. There would be those who would falsely claim to be Christ.

He stressed that *immediately after* the period of great tribulation he would return, "coming on the clouds of heaven with power and great glory". There would be nothing secret about his coming, he said, for his coming would be so obvious that it will be like lighting flashing across the sky. Everyone will see him coming. (Many years later, he told John in his Revelation that "every eye will see him".)

He went on to say that, as he comes in power and great glory, he will send out his angels to gather his elect (chosen ones). These angels would be sent out with a mighty trumpet blast, heard all over the earth.

Just before Jesus and his disciples left the Mount of Olives, Jesus warned them to be ready for that day. He told them a parable about ten virgins, all waiting for the bridegroom to come. But when the call came, "Behold, the bridegroom, come out to meet him", only five were ready to go.

Jesus told them all these things in answer to their question to him. He knew this would be the last day before his arrest.

We know from the pens of the gospel writers what happened next day: Jesus went back to the Temple, and Luke tells us that "all the people came to him in the temple to hear him". He taught them to the very last day.

In the evening, Jesus held the Passover meal with his disciples in the Upper Room. He then introduced a new element into the supper, giving them bread and wine to eat and drink. He told them that the bread represented his body, and the wine, his blood — both elements the symbol of a new covenant which would be introduced by his death.

About midnight on Thursday, they walked in the moonlight, down beside the Temple, crossed the brook Kedron and walked up to the Garden of Gethsemane on the lower slopes of the Mount of Olives. There, Jesus fought his final battle, committing himself to his Father's will.

He was arrested in the garden and crucified next morning, at 9 o'clock, and by 3 o'clock that afternoon, he was dead.

But on Sunday morning came his mighty resurrection. Through his death and resurrection, he has opened up the way of life for us.

We now wait for him to return, as he told his disciples he would, as they sat with him on the Mount of Olives.

Perhaps we will be among the crowds who throng around him again, as he enters Jerusalem on a donkey for the second time, this time as King of kings and Lord of lords. Our voices will join those of all the saints as we escort him to his throne:

> "Blessed is the King who comes in the name of the Lord! Praise in heaven and glory in the highest." (Luke 19:38)

13

The garden of Gethsemane

As we continue our journey with Jesus, our steps lead us along a path to the Garden of Gethsemane, on the lower slopes of the Mount of Olives, facing Jerusalem.

Here, we find Jesus, praying, alone. It is well past midnight. It is close to the Jewish Passover, and the moon shines overhead, its beams filtering down through the leaves of the olive trees, from whence the mountain gains its name. Here, in the moonlight, amidst the olive trees, we find Jesus.

Minutes before, the Lord had confided to Peter, James and John, "My soul is very sorrowful, even to death. Remain here and watch with me. And going a little farther, he fell on his face and prayed, 'My Father, if it be possible, let this cup pass from me. Nevertheless, not as I will, but as Thou wilt' ".

In today's language, "My Father, if it's possible, don't let me have to go through this! But I accept that it's not my wishes that must prevail, but yours".

Three times he prayed this heartfelt and desperate prayer. "Father, *all* things are possible to you. Take away this cup from me. But your will, not mine, be done".

The word's of John Stainer's *Crucifixion* bring out the pathos of these moments of bitter mental agony and trial for Jesus as he prays in that moonlit garden:

> "Jesus, Lord Jesus, bowed in bitter anguish, and bearing all the evil we
> have done. O teach us, teach us how to love you ... help us to pray, and
> watch, and mourn with thee".

Luke the physician wrote these words:

> "And there appeared to him an angel from heaven, strengthening him.
> And being in an agony, he prayed more earnestly; and his sweat became
> like great drops of blood, falling upon the ground". (Luke 22:43–44)

Jesus knew this place intimately. He had walked past this garden dozens
of times over the years since his boyhood. The main pathway from
Galilee led over the Mount of Olives and down through the garden, as
the path descended the lower slopes of the Mount opposite Jerusalem.

What do we know about the Mount of Olives?

It lies immediately east of Jerusalem. If we imagine ourselves standing
in Jerusalem on the south side of the city, we can look across and see
the Mount of Olives right in front of us, on the other side of the Kedron
Valley.

It's very close — its slope is as close as 200–300 yards from us. If we
look down, we can see the quite steep slope leading down to the brook
Kedron, just below.

Let's go for an imaginary walk.

We make our way down the path, past the Temple, to the brook, and
after crossing it, we immediately begin climbing up the slope of the
Mount of Olives. Up we go, following this main pathway, past the
Garden of Gethsemane, up to the summit. We are now about 2,700 feet
above sea level.

Down the far slope now, on the other side of the Mount. No longer
can we see Jerusalem behind us as it is hidden by the brow of the
summit. Further down we go, until we come to the two little villages
of Bethphage and Bethany. If we continued our journey, we would
continue onto Jericho, several miles away.

Back on the summit of the Mount of Olives was once a place where false
gods were worshipped. Gods such as Chemosh and Molech. Tragically,
they were worshipped there by none other than King Solomon:

> "Then Solomon built a high place for Chemosh the abomination of Moab,
> and for Molech the abomination of the Ammonites, on the mountain east

of Jerusalem. And so he did for all his foreign wives, who burned incense and sacrificed to their gods." (1 Kings 11:7–8)

Solomon also built high places for other gods on the Mount of Olives:

"And the king [Josiah] defiled the high places that were east of Jerusalem, to the south of the mount of corruption, which Solomon the king of Israel had built for Ashtoreth the abomination of the Sidonians, and for Chemosh the abomination of Moab, and for Milcom the abomination of the Ammonites." (2 Kings 23:13)

The Mount of Olives has several peaks, but there are two main peaks. These peaks slope down to a narrow saddle between the peaks, through which winds the path from Jericho to Jerusalem. Jesus knew this path through the saddle well. He had often walked up the steep path from Jericho, stopping at Bethany on the lower, eastern slopes of the Mount of Olives, and then continued up the path between the two peaks until, at the top of the saddle, there below and in front of him burst into view the city of Jerusalem on the opposite hillside.

It was at this spot that Jesus once stopped and cried out, "O Jerusalem, Jerusalem ... how often I would have gathered your children together as a hen gathers her brood under her wings and you would not".

Now, on this moonlit night, Jesus had come from Jerusalem, crossed the brook Kedron, and climbed the lower slope of the Mount of Olives until he reached the Garden of Gethsemane. For the moment, we leave him praying there while we cast our minds back over many centuries.

One thousand years earlier, another man had come to the Garden of Gethsemane. He had left Jerusalem, crossed the brook , and followed the steeply ascending path up the slope of the Mount of Olives. He had walked through the Garden of Gethsemane, for all who used that path, passed through the garden.

This man, like Jesus, was a King. He was King David. He was fleeing from Jerusalem because of his son, Absalom. We read that David

"crossed the brook Kedron, and all the people passed on toward the wilderness." (2 Samuel 15:23)

Having crossed the brook Kedron, David

"went up the ascent of the Mount of Olives, weeping as he went, barefoot and with his head covered ..." (verse 30)

This journey of David's up and over the Mount of Olives was tinged with the results of sin. His sin of adultery with Bathsheba, and the murder of her husband, Uriah, was still sending out its ripples in David's life. His son, Absalom, had rebelled against him and Absalom was being advised by Ahithophel, Bathsheba's grandfather.

It seems that Ahithophel, although a long-serving counsellor of David's, had never forgiven him for what he did to his granddaughter, Bathsheba, and her husband, Uriah.

Because of this, he found the opportunity to desert David, and crossed to the camp of Absalom. Such was the depth of Ahithophel's feeling about what had happened to Bathsheba, he advised Absalom to go into David's concubines. This was no idle advice. Absalom pitched his tent on the roof of David's palace and the concubines went into him there. This was the very roof on which David had been walking when he first saw Bathsheba. Ahithophel wanted to drive a knife into David's character by this graphic reminder of what David had done.

So, with the results of his sin clinging to him, David fled from Jerusalem — away from his son and away from the scene of his sin.

David and his men crossed the brook Kedron and began their climb up the slope of the Mount of Olives — through the Garden of Gethsemane. Turning again to Samuel's words in chapter 15:25–26 (2 Samuel), we read some astounding words:

> "If I find favour in the eyes of the Lord, He will bring me back and let me see both it (the ark) and its habitation; but if He says, 'I have no pleasure in you', behold, here I am, let Him do to me what seems good to Him."

What a remarkable thing to say! "Here I am, let Him do to me what seems good to Him." Remember the words of Jesus in this very place? "Father, not my will, but Thine, be done."

David, the man after God's own heart. Jesus, the greater son of David and Son of God. Both men committing their lives to God in the same place on the Mount of Olives.

Let's read those words again:

David: "Let Him do to me what seems good to Him"

Jesus: "Not my will, but Thine be done."

The comparison we find between David and Jesus is very significant. Consider these points:

1. David's son, Absalom, had turned against his father and became unfaithful to him as an enemy.

    God's Son loved his Father and was faithful to Him to the end.

2. Both David and Jesus were hated by the leading men of Jerusalem. Ahithophel and Absalom would have killed David if they could.

    The Jewish rulers of Jesus' time sought to kill him. Both David and Jesus on the Mount of Olives were in despair, and very sorrowful.

3. Both men committed their lives into the hand of God.

4. Both men had been betrayed by men who had been their trusted friends — Ahithophel betrayed David; Judas betrayed Jesus. Both betrayers later committed suicide.

5. Both David and Jesus were men of blood, but in a very different sense. As David went up and over the Mount of Olives, Shimai yelled at him, "Begone you man of blood, you worthless fellow", and pelted him with stones as he went along. David was indeed a man of blood — Uriah's blood.

    Jesus was also a man of blood, but not another man's blood. He shed his own blood, not that man may die, but that man might live.

So we have a picture of two men on the Mount of Olives, associated with the Garden of Gethsemane. One, David, bound up with the results of sins against Bathsheba and Uriah — "a man of blood". He placed himself in God's hands.

The other — the greater son of David, the sinless Son of God, who also put himself into God's hands. Not because of sin, but because of love and obedience. "Not my will, but Thine, be done."

1,000 years separated them. In these two men, David and Jesus, we see the flesh and the Spirit. David utters a cry of despair. Jesus utters a cry of victory — "My Father's will be done", and an angel from heaven, sent by his loving Father, ministered to him and strengthened him.

In a spiritual sense, perhaps we can perceive the Mount of Olives as a symbol of mortality and the flesh. Remember that from the Bethany side of the mount, Jerusalem cannot be seen. The rising bulk of the mount hides Jerusalem. Our mortality stands between us and the Kingdom of God, just as the Mount of Olives stands between us and Jerusalem.

There is indeed much about this mount which is reflective of the flesh and the way of the flesh. On its summit, men who should have known better worshipped false gods. David climbed its slopes with the actions of his son plunging him into despair.

We cannot forget that the victory of Jesus took place in the midst of his mortality. As he prayed fervently in the Garden of Gethsemane, on the Mount of Olives which represents mortality, victory was achieved, for he put *himself last* and *his Father first.* In his decision, "Thy will, not mine", Jesus achieved his last great victory over temptation and the flesh. He put his own will behind him.

Our own involvement with the Mount of Olives is not yet over. It still represents the way of mortality which stands between us and the Kingdom of God.

But at Jesus' return, the Mount of Olives, and mortality, will disappear, and a great wide valley will open up where the Mount of Olives now stands. The prophet, Zechariah, tells us:

> "... the Lord will go forth and fight against those nations as when he fights on a day of battle. On that day, his feet shall stand on the Mount of Olives which lies before Jerusalem on the east; and the Mount of Olives shall be split in two from east to west by a very wide valley; so that one half of the Mount shall withdraw northward, and the other half southward." (Zechariah 14:3–4)

There will be no barrier then. No longer will the view of Jerusalem be blocked by the Mount of Olives. Jerusalem will be seen by all for miles around. Gone will be the mountain — mortality — replaced by a valley leading to the new Jerusalem and the Kingdom age.

Jesus has already opened up the valley for us. Spiritually, the Mount of Olives does not hide the Kingdom of God from our spiritual view. It is our mortality which divides us from the Kingdom, and that, too, will soon be removed.

It was appropriate that Jesus ascended to heaven from the Mount of Olives. It was here that he wrought his greatest victory in the Garden of Gethsemane. His ascension from the mount symbolises the leaving behind of mortality.

When he returns, his feet will once again stand on this ancient mount of mortality. And it will split in two and disappear north and south and will be replaced by a valley with a vision of the city of the great King. At that time, the mortality of the saints will be a thing of the past.

The whole world will come to Jerusalem along this valley, with their eyes fixed on Jerusalem where Jesus will sit enthroned as King of kings and Lord of lords. As they approach Jerusalem, they will see it from far off, rising above the plain and valley, shining as a beacon of light and righteousness — the city of God and of His Son.

But today is today, and the glory of Jesus' return and the Kingdom lies ahead of us. Today, we remember and are thankful that Jesus has opened up the way of life for us, just as in the future, the Mount of Olives will open up to provide the way to Jerusalem.

We return in thought to the Garden of Gethsemane where Jesus is praying. As we contemplate his great victory over himself in the garden, we reflect that his victory came with intense suffering, because of our sin.

We remember his death on a cross, and his instruction to his followers to remember him in bread and wine, "Do this in remembrance of me."

To conclude our thoughts on the Garden of Gethsemane, the words of John Stainer in *The Crucifixion*:

> "Jesus, Lord Jesus, bowed in bitter anguish, and bearing all the evil we have done. O teach us, teach us how to love you ... help us to pray, and watch, and mourn with thee."

14

The transformation of Peter

"After they had sung a hymn, they went out to the Mount of Olives."

Jesus and his disciples had just shared together the supper in the upper room. It was very late at night, probably getting on for eleven o'clock. Judas had already disappeared into the night, and Jesus and his eleven disciples made their way in the moonlight, down beside the city wall, past the outer wall of the Temple, down the steep slope to the valley where the brook Kedron bubbled along in the moonlight.

All was still at this late hour.

Just up the hill on the other side of the brook could be seen the olive trees in the Garden of Gethsemane — dark shapes in the moonlight.

Jesus stopped beside the brook, and they all gathered around him, these eleven men. One of them standing close to Jesus was Peter.

Peter. How he loved his Lord. Only an hour or two earlier he had declared vehemently that he would never let Jesus wash *his* feet. But on being rebuked by Jesus, he had blurted out, "Lord, not only my feet, but my hands and head also."

As the disciples gathered around Jesus now, he said to them, "You will all fall away, for it is written, 'I will strike the shepherd and the sheep will be scattered.'"

What was this Jesus was saying to them? The disciples were already troubled in mind, for Jesus had told them earlier that one of them would betray him. Now he was saying they would all desert him!

What was going on? What was happening? They felt uneasy and anxious and glanced at each other in the moonlight.

Then Peter spoke up and emphatically declared, "Even if all fall away, *I* will not." Jesus looked at the big fisherman standing beside him. "This very night", Jesus replied quietly, "This very night, before the cock crows twice, you will deny me three times."

This was utterly unthinkable to Peter who loved his Lord devotedly. "Even if I have to *die* with you, I will *never* deny you", he burst out.

But only four or five hours hours later, Peter, sobbing and blinded by his bitter tears, stumbled brokenly out of the courtyard of the High Priest's house having denied his Lord, his Master, his dearest friend, not once, but three times.

He had failed to let himself be identified with Jesus. Peter, the disciple who only a few hours earlier had blurted out that he would *never* deny him. Even if he had to *die* with him, he would *never* deny him.

But he had, just as Jesus said he would, and it broke Peter. It broke him completely.

And yet, it is doubtful that we could find a greater example of a man transformed in the months that followed that incident than we have in Peter.

Six or seven months later, we again see Peter, but this time, we see him in a totally different light. The intervening months have had a profound effect upon him and have changed him completely.

We find he and John striding towards the gate of the Temple in Jerusalem. It was the gate called "Beautiful". Just outside the gate lay a crippled man. Every day, he was carried to the gate by his friends and would beg from all those who entered the Temple through the gate.

He was over forty years old, this cripple, and had never walked. He had been born a cripple. He had never known what it was like to stand up and look people in the eye from the same height. He had always looked up at people from a lying position.

As Peter and John approached, he asked them for money. This was what he always did when people approached him on the way into the Temple. Peter and John stopped, and Peter looked directly into the man's eyes. "Look at us", he commanded. The man's expectation of money increased.

> "Silver and gold I do not have, but what I have I give to you. In the name of Jesus Christ of Nazareth, walk".

Here was a changed Peter! No longer broken in spirit, he had been transformed. There was no denying Jesus now. Openly, he proclaimed his Lord. "In the name of Jesus Christ ..."

And there was no denying that Jesus was alive. Miracles are not performed in the name of a dead man.

Peter held out his hand to the man, and he leaped to his feet. No struggling up having to be supported once he was up. No tentative, unconfident, staggering to his feet here. Acts 3:7–8 are explosive in their description of how this man was healed:

> "And he (Peter) took him by the right hand and raised him up; and *immediately*, his feet and ankles were made strong. And *leaping up*, he stood and walked and entered the Temple with them, *walking and leaping and praising God*." (Italics added)

People from all over the Temple came running to see what the shouting was all about. They were astonished and amazed to see the crippled man they had known for years, leaping and jumping and shouting praise to God.

What did Peter do? He saw that here was an opportunity to proclaim the name of Jesus Christ and that he was alive. He had been killed, crucified on a cross, but was now alive again. He told the swelling crowds that they had killed Jesus, the author of life, but God had raised him from the dead, and he, Peter, had seen and spoken to the risen Lord.

For three hours he preached to them. In that three hours, and again before the Sanhedrin the next morning, he constantly told them that Jesus was risen and alive. Chapters 3 and 4 of Acts has five references to the fact that Jesus was alive, and six references to the name of Jesus Christ. And those chapters obviously contain only a fraction of what Peter said in those three hours.

It is important to grasp that the particular aspect of this dramatic event is that in it, we see a Peter who was totally transformed. He taught and preached in the name of Jesus Christ with power and utmost conviction. He was able to do that because he was a changed man.

All of us who have committed ourselves to follow Jesus are kept very busy in our lives of service to him. It is an important part of our discipleship that we preach the gospel, minister to one another, be involved in Sunday School work, support Mission activities, give time to looking after our aged loved ones. Welfare work, youth activities, bible classes, study weekends, preaching weekends, bible schools, bringing up our families — all of these activities and much more are all a most important part of our life in Christ Jesus.

But although all of these things are important in serving the Lord, they are not our primary goal in this life. They may assist us in achieving our primary goal, but they are secondary to that goal.

The principle requirement that God asks of us as His sons and daughters, is the one thing that is hardest for us to achieve. He asks us to overcome ourselves. That is our primary goal. He asks us to change. He asks us to be transformed. He wants to lift us from the ways of the flesh and mortality, to the ways of the Spirit and immortality. In asking this, he asks us to swim against the tide of our own nature. He asks us to go against the grain of our natural inclinations. And He promises that when we stumble and fail in our efforts, He will forgive us, for Jesus' sake.

He asks us to put behind us our human nature, and, through the strength which comes through the Lord Jesus Christ, become like Christ. He asks us to change. He asks us to be transformed.

> "Do not be conformed to this world", wrote Paul to those in Rome, "but be transformed by the renewal of your mind ..." (Romans 12:2)

This is the first and greatest responsibility of every follower of the Lord Jesus. If our lives, out temperaments, our characters have not changed in the years we have been in Christ; if our hearts have not been softened, and if the peace of God has not quenched the fires of our human nature, then our life in Christ has been in vain.

There is only one way any of us can be transformed, and that is for our hearts to be touched and filled by Jesus. If the knowledge of the gospel has not got beyond our head to our heart, then we are as clanging gongs and crashing cymbals — producing much noise but no music.

There is an old hymn, written by James Duffill, with music by A.J. Gordon, which reflects the love for Jesus which comes from a changed heart:

> "My Jesus, I love thee, I know thou art mine;
> For thee, all the follies of sin I resign;
> My gracious Redeemer, my Saviour art thou!
> If ever I loved thee, my Jesus, 'tis now."

When Jesus sent his message to the seven ecclesias through his Revelation, he didn't say:

> "He that does better works I will make a pillar in the temple of my God."

Or

> "He who gains the most converts through preaching, I will grant to sit with me on my throne."

No, he didn't say that. He promised rewards to everyone of the members of those seven ecclesias who overcame themselves.

"He who overcomes ..." was his plea to them. They were to overcome themselves. They were to become changed people. They were to experience the transformation which comes from a heart and mind which is changed by the love of Jesus Christ and forgiveness of sins through him.

It seems that the ecclesia at Laodicea contained members whose hearts had not been transformed, or if they once had, they had allowed themselves to be pulled back to the world. Otherwise, Jesus would not have described them as lukewarm. "Because you are lukewarm, and neither cold nor hot, I will spew you out of my mouth", said Jesus.

Peter's transformation occurred after the Lord's resurrection. Our thoughts return to those dreadful hours before his death, in the courtyard of the house of the High Priest. At this time, Peter had not yet been transformed, though he loved his Lord dearly.

We find Peter inside this courtyard, having been let in there by a servant girl at the gate. It was about 3 am and bitterly cold. Peter was not keen to be recognised, but there is something about him which attracts the attention of this girl. "You also were with Jesus of Galilee."

"I don't know what you're talking about", snapped a nervous Peter.

There was no going back now. He had refused to identify himself with Jesus.

Then, about an hour later, as Peter tried to get warm by the courtyard fire, another girl exclaimed, "This fellow *was* with Jesus of Nazareth."

"I don't *know* the man!"

What was Peter thinking in his heart as he blurted out these words of denial? He was in a one-way street now, and there was no way he could go back. He was in the courtyard at great risk to himself, because of his love for his Master. Yet, twice now, he had absolutely denied any association with him.

An hour passes. "Surely you *are* one of them, for your Galilean accent gives you away."

Peter, completely unnerved now, cursed and swore and shouted and yelled, "*I don't know the man.*"

Then two things happened. First, the cock crowed for the second time. Second, unnoticed by Peter, Jesus had been led into the courtyard, bound. And in the midst of his cursing and swearing and denial of the man he loved most of all, Peter suddenly noticed Jesus standing there. *He had heard every word!*

It is Luke who penned those seven poignant words:

"The Lord turned and looked at Peter."

What was in that look? Was it sadness or disappointment in Peter? Was it a look of reproach? Or was it a look of reassurance and forgiveness by the Lord, who knew Peter's heart through and through?

Looking into Jesus' eyes in those few seconds, a repentance greater than he had ever experienced welled up in Peter's heart. It was more than he could bear. He had denied Jesus, but Jesus had not denied him.

He ran from the courtyard, weeping as if his pent-up heart would break.

But it was those same eyes of the risen Jesus which, three days later, looked into Peter's eyes again. We know nothing of what took place between them. It is not recorded. We know only that Jesus appeared to Peter. (Luke 24:34) In that private meeting with his risen Lord, Peter was transformed.

The same Jesus who we remember in bread and wine each week, lifted Peter from his morass of misery and guilt to a life transformed. He can do that for us, too. If Christ dwells in our hearts every day, he will lift us, as he did Peter, and we will be transformed:

> "May Christ dwell in our hearts through faith; rooted and grounded in love, having the power to comprehend with all the saints what is the breadth, and length and height and depth, and to know the love of Christ which surpasses knowledge, being filled with all the fullness of God." (Ephesians 3:17–19)

15

Behold, the lamb of God

It was early on the morning of the day before Passover — about 8 am. Just outside the wall of Jerusalem, a crowd made their noisy way to a spot they called "The Place of the Skull".

This was no ordinary crowd. There were Roman soldiers escorting three men to be crucified. As they made their way to the Place of the Skull, crowds swarmed about them, eager to see what was going on. News spread like wildfire through the crowded city — "Jesus of Nazareth has been arrested! They are going to crucify him!"

His followers couldn't believe their ears. Jesus! The young prophet who had healed hundreds of them, who had even raised at least three people from death to life. The man they expected to become their king. Surely there was a mistake.

They ran towards the Place of the Skull. Hundreds of others were there as well. The crowds were thick, even this early in the morning. "Keep back!", yelled the soldiers. "Get over there and keep well back from the crosses." But a young man who said he was Jesus' cousin John went up to the soldiers and asked if Jesus' mother and relatives, and his close friend, Mary, could come close to where Jesus was to be crucified Permission was granted.

It is hard for us, two thousand years later, living in a western civilisation, to even begin to imagine the noise, tumult and emotion of that day. Shouting men, Roman soldiers bellowing out orders and trying to achieve some semblance of order, curious onlookers trying to get a glimpse of the three prisoners — especially the one called ... Jesus of Nazareth.

Representatives of the Jewish leaders were there. Their job was to make sure that the job was done. They stood back a little way from the cross, jeering and sarcastic as Jesus staggered between the soldiers and approached the Place of the Skull. Revengeful and hard-hearted, these men looked on with gimlet eyes as they shouted their jibes at the bleeding and wounded Jesus. At last they had him! Not long now and he would be dead — no longer a problem for them.

There were men and women there, too, who were not curious, but heart-broken. Those who were allowed close to the cross of Jesus, his mother Mary, her sister, Salome, Salome's son, John, Mary, the wife of Cleopas, who was probably also Jesus' aunt, and Mary Magdalene.

Standing further back, at the insistence of the Roman soldiers, were others who were also heart-broken — men and women whom Jesus had healed and who had heard his message of the Kingdom of God gladly. Standing there, they wept openly at this terrible thing happening to their master and teacher.

Perhaps the man who had been born blind was there — the one whom Jesus healed, and as a result the man was cast out of the Temple. Jesus had found him, and had comforted him. Almost certainly Lazarus was there, and his sisters Mary and Martha. Maybe the parents of the children whom Jesus had held in his arms were there, too.

And some of the ten lepers whom Jesus had healed. These, and many others, would be there, for people from all over Israel had come to Jerusalem for the annual Passover. There were tens of thousands in the city on that day.

In the centre of this scene of intense drama and human suffering was Jesus himself. The one whom Isaiah had described seven hundred years earlier:

> "He was despised and rejected by men; a man of sorrows and acquainted with grief ... he was despised, and we esteemed him not." (Isaiah 53:3)

Dreadful though that scene at the cross was, we cannot remember Jesus' agony and suffering in the context of the cross alone. The ordeal of the actual crucifixion was in fact the culmination of a life of rejection by his own people.

A little over three years earlier, his cousin, John the Baptist, had stood on the banks of the Jordan River with two men. As they talked together, John saw Jesus approaching and said to the two men, "Behold, the Lamb of God."

One wonders whether these two men grasped the import of those words at the time — "Behold, the Lamb of God." Whether they did or not, from that time on, Jesus was a marked man. Not because John had called him "the Lamb of God", but because as the days and weeks and months progressed, Jesus' influence over the people became increasingly obvious. The Jewish leaders quickly perceived him as a threat to their authority.

He met constant and growing opposition from these Jewish leaders, and his life was in constant danger. We read in the gospels phrases such as:

"This was why the Jews sought all the more to kill him."

"The chief priests and Pharisees sent officers to arrest him."

"From that day on, they took counsel how to put him to death."

Finally, at the end of his ministry, he met with his disciples alone, in the upper room. Even there, one of his disciples was a betrayer. Jesus' words to Judas were, "What you are about to do, do quickly." Judas immediately went out, and, as John poignantly puts it, "It was night."

In the moonlit darkness of that night, Jesus and his eleven remaining disciples walked the half mile or so from the upper room, down the steep, narrow track at the edge of the city leading down to the brook Kedron. Crossing the brook, they walked up the hill on the other side of the brook into the Garden of Gethsemane on the slopes of the Mount of Olives.

So began the last hours of Jesus' suffering which were to culminate at Golgotha, the Place of the Skull.

We can but glimpse the inner struggle Jesus had there in the garden, alone. It was a struggle he could not even share with his three closest disciples, Peter, James and John. He left them, and went a little way from them, but Mark writes that even before he left them, he "began to be greatly distressed and troubled."

This was not like Jesus. One gets the impression right through his ministry, and certainly during the terrible hours after his arrest, that he steadfastly kept his own feelings deeply within himself, and outwardly appeared as a man of calmness and inner strength. But here, with the disciples he loved most close by, he allowed his human feelings to show, and was greatly distressed and troubled.

Jesus knew what lay ahead. Had he not said to his disciples in the upper room, "I have desired to eat this feast with you *before I suffer*?" His knowledge of the Old Testament scriptures would leave no doubt in his mind what lay ahead, and it was not just the agony of the cross. But it had to be borne alone.

In the Garden of Gethsemane, the awesome burden of this aloneness was almost more than Jesus could bear. Luke 22:42 gives us Jesus' agonised plea to his Father, "Father, if you are willing, remove this cup from me ... "

Luke the physician records that "being in an agony he prayed more earnestly, and his sweat became like great drops of blood falling down upon the ground."

Let us pause a moment to consider what was happening here. This condition in which blood is mingled with sweat is known medically as haematidrosis. It only occurs when severe suffering is being experienced, to the extent that the body reacts physically under the strain. The blood capillaries just under the skin swell and dilate so much that they come into contact with the sweat glands. When this happens, the blood capillaries burst and the blood mixes with the sweat as it runs off the body. Such was the severity of the suffering of Jesus, that he suffered haematidrosis.

His deep distress is reflected in Hebrews:

> "When he had offered up prayers and supplications with strong crying and tears unto Him that was able to save him from death, he was heard in that he feared; though he were a son, yet learned he obedience by the things which he suffered ... " (Hebrews 5:7–8)

Immediately, an angel came to him, strengthening him.

Then came the arrest. The next few hours show us human nature at its worst. Cowards become cruel when they have the upper hand. The

Jewish leaders, now that they had Jesus under arrest, played out their revenge to the full.

By now, it was well past midnight — probably about 3 am. Jesus had had no sleep that night, nor would he get any. Every act of cruelty and torture imposed upon Jesus in these hours after his arrest were prophesied in detail in the scriptures. Jesus would have been acutely aware of those prophecies. Here are a few examples:

> "I gave my back to the smiters, and my cheek to those who pulled out the beard; I hid not my face from shame and spitting." (Isaiah 50:6)

> "He was wounded for our transgressions, he was bruised for our iniquities ... with his stripes we are healed." (Isaiah 53:5)

> "He was oppressed, and he was afflicted, yet he opened not his mouth; like a lamb that is led to the slaughter, and like a sheep before its shearers is dumb, so he opened not his mouth." (Isaiah 53:7)

Jesus knew that all of this applied to him. He knew that he must go through this agony. Consider the awful fulfilment of these prophecies in what happened to Jesus during the night — he was struck blows, stripped of his clothes, scourged, people spat in his face, he was blindfolded, slapped, jeered at, mocked, he had a crown of sharp thorns rammed onto his head and made to wear a scarlet robe.

Let us not be under any misapprehension. Jesus was beaten up. He suffered a hiding at the hands of these Jewish leaders who were out for revenge. And the Roman soldiers added their contribution, mocking him, kneeling in front of him, saying "Hail, king of the Jews." They, too, slapped him and spat on him. Then they whipped his back and sides to a pulp with a violent Roman scourging. No wonder Isaiah had prophesied seven hundred years earlier:

> "As many were astonished at him — his appearance was so marred, beyond human semblance, and his form beyond that of the sons of men ..." (Isaiah 52:14)

Tracing his movements through the gospels, we find that Jesus, his hands bound, was first taken to the house of Annas, the father of Caiaphas, the High Priest. No doubt the Temple soldiers treated him pretty roughly on the way, although we are not told that. We are told, however, that at Annas's house, he was struck by a Jewish officer with the hand (John 18:22). The Diaglott states that "one of the officers standing by gave Jesus a blow, saying, "Is that the way you answer the High Priest?"

Annas sent him to Caiaphas, still bound. It was while he was with Caiaphas that the Jewish leaders struck him with more blows, mocked him, spat in his face, beat him, blindfolded him and reviled him. What revenge they enjoyed! How they had longed to do this to Jesus.

By now, it doesn't take much imagination to envisage what condition Jesus was in. It was approaching dawn. He had had no sleep for about twenty four hours. He had sweated freely in the garden and blood had run down his face with the sweat. He was bruised on his face and body by the slaps, blows and punches and his face had spittle running down it. *Remember, he was bound, and could not even wipe his face.* No one was there to wipe it for him.

"I hid not my face from shame and spitting." (Isaiah 50:6)

Caiaphas then sends him, still bound, to Pilate, at the Praetorium. Pilate, after questioning him, sends him to Herod. Herod and his soldiers treated Jesus with contempt, and mocked him and arrayed him in gorgeous apparel and made fun of him. Jesus uttered not one single word to Herod.

Herod sent him back to Pilate, where the whole battalion of Pilate's soldiers stripped him of his clothes, placed a purple robe on him, and a crown of thorns, and mocked him. They, too, punched him with blows to the body and spat on him.

After they had done all this, Pilate brought him out and displayed him to all the people, arrayed in the purple robe and wearing the crown of thorns, and said, "Behold the man."

And they would behold Jesus, probably barely able to stand after the beatings he'd had, bruised all over his body, with dried blood and spittle on his face. "Behold the man."

What ignorance on Pilate's part! He had no idea of Jesus' real identity. Three years earlier, John the Baptist had proclaimed, "Behold the Lamb of God." And here was Pilate, presenting to the people, this same man who his soldiers and Temple guards had belted up several times, spat on him and left him in a pitiful state, with the words, "Behold the man."

Think about these words. Not "Behold the *man*", but "*Behold* the man." In effect, Pilate was saying to the Jews, "Look at him. Is it this belted up specimen who you want for your king?"

We live in a world whose occupants deny the Lord Jesus Christ, who reject him, who use his name blasphemously. We live in a world in which things of the Spirit are not perceived or acknowledged. We live in a world of fleshly pursuits and attitudes.

The world was no different in Pilate's day. He, like those in the world today, could not see beyond the flesh. It was beyond them to see that this man was the Son of God. In Pilate's limited vision, Jesus was a beaten-up specimen of humanity and nothing else. "*Behold* the man." Like all about him, he could see no further that superficiality. How spiritually blind was Pilate and the Jewish leaders who waited for his verdict. They could see no further than the man presented before them.

After all this, Pilate had Jesus scourged. We recall Isaiah's words, "He gave his back to the smiters." For that is what scourging entailed — a violent whipping across the back of the victim, using a whip made of several thongs of leather with a piece of chain or bone attached to each thong.

The scourging alone would render any man almost physically immobile. Some men died during the whipping. A Roman scourging on top of what Jesus had already suffered would have left him in a dreadful state. His back would be terribly lacerated, blood would be pouring from his wounds steadily weakening him from loss of blood, he was exhausted, filthy, humiliated and rejected:

> "Thou knowest my reproach, and my shame, and my dishonour. My foes are all known to Thee. Insults have broken my heart, so that I am in despair. I looked for pity, but there was none; and for comforters, but I found none." (Psalm 69:19–20)

In this dreadful and pitiful condition, Jesus commences his painful, almost impossible, walk to Golgotha through the streets of Jerusalem. Small wonder the soldiers compelled Simon of Cyrene to carry his cross. Jesus, by this time, would have barely been able to walk. Carrying a heavy piece of timber was quite beyond him. John tells us that he started out carrying the cross, but didn't get very far with it.

Although Simon of Cyrene didn't grasp the fact at the time, what a unique privilege it was to carry the cross of the Son of God. No-one else was granted that privilege. One wonders whether this experience changed Simon's life and if he became a follower of Jesus.

Then ... Golgotha, the place of a skull. John writes so simply of this momentous event for mankind; this awful climax in the suffering of our Lord:

> "So they took Jesus ... to the place called the place of a skull which is called in Hebrew, 'Golgotha'. There they crucified him." (John 19:17–18)

Here, at the foot of the cross, we rejoin those faithful five amidst the uproar and shouting and jeering. But in this black turmoil of hatred and bitterness, with human nature baying like wolves, there shines through it all the light of love and faith on that day of agony. Love which was manifest in the love of a Father for His Son, and the love of a Son for his Father. Love which is exemplified in those wonderful words of John the Baptist's"

> "Behold the Lamb of God."

For, as those faithful ones at the foot of the cross looked up to see their beloved Jesus hanging there, close to death, lacerated, swollen, bruised and bleeding, those words of John the Baptist's took on their full meaning, even if they were too grief-stricken to realise it at that moment.

Fifteen hundred years earlier, God had decreed which animals were to be offered as a sin offering. In the case of the High Priest and the nation as a whole, a bullock was to offered. In the case of a ruler, a male goat was to be offered. For one of the common people, a female goat or lamb was to be the sacrifice. If the people could not afford an animal for sacrifice, they were permitted to offer turtle doves or pigeons, or if they could not afford those, they could offer a tenth of an ephah of fine flour.

But *no-one* was permitted to provide a male lamb as a sin offering. This right was reserved for God alone. Jesus was that lamb — the Lamb of God.

Oh, shades of the hill of Moriah so long before — "My father, where is the lamb for a burnt offering?", Isaac asked Abraham. "God will provide Himself the lamb, my son", was Abraham's reply.

We are those sinners for whom this sacrifice of the Lamb of God was made. Because of this sacrifice of God's own Son, we have forgiveness of sins. It is because of this suffering and sacrifice, we can pray for forgiveness:

> "God so loved the world that He gave His only Son, that whoever believes in him should not perish but have eternal life." (John 3:16)

The death of Jesus has a deeply personal effect on all who accept him as their Saviour. The apostle Paul expressed this personal feeling in his letter to the Galatians:

> "The life I now live in the flesh I live by faith in the Son of God, who loved me, and gave himself for me." (Galatians 2:20)

The beautiful and deeply moving words of a hymn by L.G. Sargent express this same personal relationship to our Lord:

> "Was it for me thy flesh was wounded sore,
> Thy body lifted high on cross of shame?
> Was it for me the King of glory bore
> So meek the scourge, and ruthless men's defame?
>
> Was there no way for any man to live
> But thou must die, no joy but through thy grief?
> Is sin so dark that God cannot forgive
> Save through thy sacrifice, and our belief?
>
> Lord, let me learn thy sorrow, mark thy pain,
> That no more heedless through the world I roam,
> But come to take the pardon thou didst gain,
> And find within thy fold, eternal home."

We rejoice that this same Lamb gave us the words of Revelation. He will be in the midst of the throne of the Kingdom of God. He is not only the Lamb, but also our shepherd, and there will come a time when he will rule from that ancient throne of David, in Jerusalem. At that time there will no more hunger, no more thirst, no more suffering, no more death, for "he will guide us to springs of living water, and will wipe away every tear from our eyes."

He it is who can disentangle the complications of our lives, lift us from the morasses of our sin, free us from the constraints of our guilt, and lift us ultimately from mortality to immortality.

16

The clothes of the high priest

Clothes are mentioned quite often in the pages of scripture.

The first clothing of course were fig leaves, worn by Adam and Eve, and then skins of animals:

> **"The Lord God made for Adam and for his wife garments of skins, and clothed them." (Genesis 3:21)**

This was the first occasion when animals were killed because of sin — the sin of Adam and Eve. In a spiritual figure, in baptism we put on the cloak of righteousness of our Lord Jesus, who died, sinless like those animals, because of our sin.

We know that Joseph had a special article of clothing — a special robe given to him by his father:

> "Now, Jacob loved Joseph more than any other of his children ... and he made him a long robe with sleeves." (Genesis 37:3)

This robe was to engender hatred and deceit against Joseph by his brothers. This was not the first time in Jacob's family that clothes were associated with deception and hatred. Jacob's mother, Rebekah, had urged him to put on his brother, Esau's, garments to deceive his father, Isaac. Isaac was taken in by Jacob's deceit. And the result? Hatred and envy by Esau against Jacob, and a determination to kill him at the first opportunity.

In our own lives, clothing plays an important part in presenting ourselves to the world. Hence the old saying, "Clothes maketh the man." We observe certain customs in our dress. Hospital workers often wear white coats, boiler attendants wear blue overalls, bus drivers used to wear grey dust coats. We wear different clothes to a barbeque than we would to an orchestral concert. Fire fighters wear yellow overalls so they can be easily seen through the smoke.

In Joseph's case, his special robe made his brothers hate him. He was wearing the robe when he went to find his brothers at Dothan. They looked up and saw him coming, and they saw that he was wearing that special robe, and they hated him for it. They hated him because of his dreams and because they thought he seemed to think of himself as someone special. They hated him because he was his father's favourite — the first son of Jacob's beloved Rachel.

In fact, Joseph was a strikingly good looking young man, and a person of above average intelligence. Josephus, the Jewish historian, writes that Jacob "loved him above the rest of his sons, both because of the beauty of his body and the virtues of his mind, for he excelled the rest (of his brothers) in prudence."

The scriptures confirm this, and describe Joseph as "handsome and good looking ... " This was how the wife of Potiphar saw him, and we find another garment coming into the picture. Joseph was wearing a cloak when Potiphar's wife asked him to lie with her, but Joseph fled, leaving his cloak in her hands.

But let's return to Joseph and his brothers. When they saw Joseph approaching them at Dothan, they at first decided to kill him, then thought better of it, and decided to cast him into a deep pit:

> "Then Judah said to his brothers, 'What profit is it if we slay our brother and conceal his blood? Come, let us sell him to the Ishmaelites, and let not our hand be upon him, for he is our brother, our own flesh. And his brothers heeded him. Then Midian traders passed by; and they drew Joseph up and lifted him out of the pit, and sold him to the Ishmaelites for twenty pieces of silver; and they took Joseph to Egypt." (Genesis 37:26–28)

We find from Genesis 37:23–24 that "when Joseph came to his brothers, they stripped him of his robe, the long robe with sleeves that he wore, and they took him and cast him into a pit."

What did they do with his robe after they stripped him of it? No doubt they flung it down beside the pit while they lowered Joseph into the pit. Later, after they had sent Joseph on his way to Egypt, they picked it up and soaked it in goat's blood and took it back to Jacob.

There was another robe, seventeen hundred years later, which was thrown down at the foot of a cross, just as the brothers of Joseph had thrown down his robe beside the pit.

Let's pick up the details of this scene at the cross. We know that after Pilate had scourged Jesus, he handed him over to his soldiers to take him away and crucify him. But before the soldiers actually took him to the crucifixion site, they took Jesus into Pilate's palace, known as the Praetorium.

At this point, Jesus was suffering enormously from the effects of the scourging he'd received. Just consider the situation:

- He'd been up all the night before.
- During that night, he'd been taken before the chief priests and elders and tried, and found guilty of blasphemy.
- He was then taken to Pilate, who questioned him.
- He was taken across to another part of the city to be questioned by King Herod. Herod was amazed that Jesus spoke not one word to him. He didn't answer any of Herod's questions.
- In the darkness of this same night, Herod sent him back to Pilate.
- Pilate, under great pressure from the Jewish leaders, scourged Jesus and ordered that he be crucified.

Not only was Jesus physically and mentally exhausted, but he'd been beaten up by the soldiers and now whipped with a flagellum. Physical shock, extreme pain and loss of blood from his back, torn to ribbons by the flagellum, would have caused him to be barely conscious, as he was led into the Praetorium after his scourging. In the Praetorium, the whole Roman battalion was assembled. These men would be the personal bodyguard of Pilate.

The soldiers stripped Jesus of his clothes and replaced them with a scarlet or purple robe. Imagine the agony of removing the clothing. They would be sticking to the raw wounds on his back and sides, the blood having dried. The clothes would have to be ripped from his wounds.

Then they mocked him, and placed a crown of thorns on his head, and spat on him, and cried out, "Hail, king of the Jews!":

> "Then the soldiers of the governor took Jesus into the Praetorium, and they gathered the whole battalion before him. And they stripped him and put a scarlet robe upon him, and plaiting a crown of thorns they put it on his head, and put a reed in his right hand. And kneeling before him they mocked him, saying, 'Hail, king of the Jews!' And they spat upon him, and took the reed and struck him on the head." (Matthew 27:27–30)

Verse 31 tells us that they took the scarlet robe off him and put his own clothes back on him. Note carefully, "they put his own clothes on him." It is also worth noting the soldiers put his clothes on him. Jesus would be too weak to dress himself.

So we find that as Jesus set out on his painful and staggering journey to **Golgotha,** *he was wearing his own clothes*. This is important.

William Barclay writes that every Jewish man wore five articles of clothing:

- Shoes
- A turban
- A girdle
- An inner garment
- An outer cloak or robe

When they arrived at the scene of the crucifixion, ***they once again stripped him of his clothes.*** These were thrown in a heap in front of the cross. The two others crucified beside him, one on each side, would have had their clothes piled in a heap in front of their crosses. We recall Joseph, when they had stripped him of *his* robe, and threw it down beside the pit.

There were five articles of clothing. There were four soldiers present. They divided four of the articles between the soldiers (one each). Who was to have the fifth garment — the robe of Jesus?

It was a special robe, woven without seam, woven from top to bottom. So they cast lots for it. This was a perfect fulfilment of Psalm 22:18:

> "They divide my garments among them, and for my raiment, they cast lots."

Let's pause a moment to check these facts against scripture:

"When the soldiers had crucified Jesus, they took his garments and made four parts, one for each soldier; also his tunic. But the tunic was without seam, woven from top to bottom; so they said to one another, 'Let us not tear it, but cast lots for it to see whose it shall be." (John 19:23–24)

Close by, at the foot of the cross, stood his mother Mary, his aunt, Salome, Mary, wife of Cleopas, thought by historians to be another aunt, his cousin, John and Mary Magdalene, his close friend.

We can imagine how Mary his mother was feeling as the soldiers calmly divided his clothes amongst them. The agony and indignity of crucifixion was almost more than a mother could bear. To see the soldiers seizing her son's very clothes and dividing them amongst them, must have been awful for her.

And the robe. Where had Jesus got that robe? We don't know, but it was the sort of robe his mother may have made for him. Or perhaps Mary Magdalene had made it for him. It was without seam, woven from top to bottom. It was specially made.

Unlike Joseph's robe, there is no record of what happened to the robe of Jesus. The fascinating book, *The Robe*, by Lloyd Douglas, is a fictional story of the robe, wonderfully told, but scripture is silent about what happened to it after one of the soldiers had won it by lot.

Why is there so much emphasis on Jesus' clothes? We have seen that Psalm 22 prophesies that lots would be cast for his robe, and this is mentioned by John in its fulfilment. We are told in some detail about Jesus' clothes being removed in the Praetorium and then his own clothes put back on him; and finally, we are told that his own clothes were removed at the cross.

John tells us (John 19:40) that his dead body was bound in linen cloths, with spices, as is the burial custom of the Jews. It was also customary to wrap a linen cloth or napkin around the head. This was how Jesus was buried, in accordance with the custom, and in accordance with the Law of Moses.

Our thoughts go forward now to the morning of resurrection, when the astonished and bewildered women and disciples found that the body of Jesus was not in the tomb. The women came first to the empty tomb, and then, summoned by Mary Magdalene, Peter and John ran to the tomb. Peter went in first, and John (20:6) tells us that he saw the linen burial cloths lying, and the napkin rolled up in a place by itself. **We should note particularly the emphasis on these two items of burial cloths.**

So when Jesus left the tomb, he left behind the linen cloths in which he had been wrapped. In these discarded linen cloths, we have a great spiritual event.

Under the Mosaic Law, we know it was the duty of the High Priest to go into the Holy Place once each year. It is especially interesting to note that he had to wear special clothes before he went into the Holy Place. Thus, before he entered, he had to change from his ordinary clothes to these special clothes:

> "Thus shall Aaron come into the Holy Place ... He shall put on the holy linen coat, and shall have the linen breeches on his body, be girded with the linen girdle, and wear the linen turban; these are the holy garments." (Leviticus 16:4)

We see from the Law that the High Priest wore linen clothes and had a linen turban on his head. When he left the Holy Place, Aaron the High Priest had to take off those clothes *before he left the Holy Place and leave them there:*

> "Then Aaron shall come into the tent of meeting, and shall put off the linen garments which he put on when he went into the Holy Place, and shall leave them there." (Leviticus 16:23)

Why did the High Priest have to leave behind the clothes he wore when he entered the Holy Place? In entering the Holy Place each year, the High Priest was the instrument of change. Atonement and forgiveness of sin brings change — change from sinfulness to cleansing. The forgiveness of our sin changes us in God's sight.

God cannot look upon sin. To have an open relationship with God, we must first have our sins forgiven. So there is a change in our state, in our condition, because of forgiveness of our sins.

The leaving behind of the High Priest's clothes when he left the Holy Place, was an indication of the change that took place through his atoning work. By leaving behind the clothes he went in with, and coming out with new clothes, he symbolised this change which atonement brings.

Jesus, through his death, made atonement for us. Not with the blood of a goat, but his own blood. The blood which flowed from his body as he hung and died on the cross.

There is only one way sin can be forgiven — through the shedding of blood.

> "Without the shedding of blood there is no forgiveness of sin." (Hebrews 9:22)

No-one but Jesus could have entered that tomb, dead, and have come out again alive. He was clothed in linen clothes, just as the High Priest was. When he came out, he left those linen clothes behind in the tomb. His death, with its atoning effect, was the work of our great High Priest. He went into the tomb of death and atonement dressed in linen clothes. He came out and left them behind in the tomb.

But Jesus came out of the tomb wearing new clothes — just as the High Priest did. Where did Jesus get those clothes? There can only be one answer to that question. They were provided by his Father, who raised him to life from death. Whether the clothes were brought to him by an angel, or whether God caused them to be there for Jesus to put on when he was resurrected, or whether God Himself raised His Son from the dead, we don't know. But without doubt, his clothes could only have been provided for him by his Father.

What does it now matter what happened to the clothes he was wearing just before he was crucified? Those clothes, even his special robe, served their purpose and have now vanished into history.

How much more important were the clothes provided for him as he rose to life and immortality? His new clothes were a symbol of the great change wrought through the shedding of his own blood.

Now we can see why such emphasis is laid on Jesus' clothes. As our great High Priest, the routine of correct clothing as prescribed under God's principles in the Law was followed exactly.

In our new life, when Jesus returns to take us to himself, there will be new clothes for us to wear, too:

> "Hallelujah! For the Lord our God the Almighty reigns. Let us rejoice and exult and give Him the glory, for the marriage of the Lamb has come, and his bride has made herself ready; it was granted to her to be clothed

with fine linen, bright and pure, for the fine linen is the righteous deeds of the saints." (Revelation 19:6–8)

May we use the time that remains before that great day to make ourselves ready, so that as the waiting bride of Jesus, we will respond joyfully and instantly when we hear the words of his angel:

"Behold, the Bridegroom! Come out to meet him."

And we will do so, to be clothed with the garments of immortality, provided for us by Jesus himself.

17

The risen Lord

The death of Jesus was accompanied by staggering circumstances. The whole of Jerusalem was on a razor edge of tension and turmoil.

The events during the night before Jesus' crucifixion were not known to the common people. The Jewish leaders had deliberately chosen the hours of darkness to arrest him and try him. In the early hours of the day before the Passover, they led him out to be crucified. It was first thing in the morning before the people in the city heard about Jesus' arrest during the night, and many didn't hear of his crucifixion until he was hanging on the cross.

There were thousands of people in Jerusalem from all over Israel. It was the time of the Passover, and the city was packed with people. Hundreds, thousands of these people were devoted followers of Jesus. Many of them had been healed by him. A few had even been raised from death by him. Most had heard him speak of the coming Kingdom of God. In the face of religious self-centredness by their religious leaders, the common people, we are told, "heard him gladly."

Was the young man who Jesus raised from the dead at Nain there in Jerusalem? Very likely. Were the two blind men from Jericho there? It was only six days ago that Jesus had healed their blindness. Was the man who had been paralysed there? Jesus had healed him after his friends let him down through the roof. And what about the man who he had healed of dropsy in the Capernaum synagogue, or the woman taken in adultery whose sin Jesus forgave, or the cripple he had healed at the pool of Bethesda?

All these people, and many more, were there in Jerusalem that day. What were their thoughts when they heard the dreadful news that Jesus had been crucified?

Let's try and reconstruct the circumstances in Jerusalem at that time.

Whether they had heard about the crucifixion or not, every single person in Jerusalem that day was aware that something abnormal and frightening was happening. It was gradually growing darker and darker. Luke records that about the sixth hour (12 noon) "there was darkness over the whole land until the ninth hour" This by itself would be enough to create fear and alarm among the people.

What did the Roman soldiers think of this growing darkness? Or the Temple guards? Or the Jewish leaders? It lasted for three hours, and Luke tells us that the sun's light failed. Stars were visible, it was necessary for lights to be lit at midday.

Then, at 3pm (the ninth hour), something else happened which struck terror into the hearts of everyone in Jerusalem. A great earthquake shook the city. It happened at the exact time that Jesus cried out with a loud voice, and died.

Great rocks split in two, Matthew tells us. The whole city was violently shaken, as in the unnatural darkness which brooded over the land, the whole of Jerusalem heaved and shook because of the earthquake. People were dumbfounded with astonishment as the earthquake opened old tombs. Three days later, after Jesus' resurrection, people who had been dead and buried in these tombs came out of them — alive again, and went into the city and appeared to many.

The Jewish leaders were aghast and worried by the fact that the curtain of the Temple was ripped in two, from top to bottom, by no human hand. Their anxiety increased over the next twenty-four hours as, according to historians of the time, there were real signs of revolt among the people because Jesus had been killed. The leaders were seriously worried that, once the Sabbath was over, they would have a serious rebellion on their hands.

On the Sabbath day, they went to the governor, Pontius Pilate,, and asked him to place a guard of soldiers at the tomb, to prevent any attempt by the people to steal the body of Jesus, and to quell any uprising after the Sabbath.

So, the Sabbath day came to its end. The disciples and the women who had been at the crucifixion were grief stricken and shattered. The women planned to return to the tomb and anoint his body as soon as the Sabbath was over. It was the last thing these devoted women could do for their Lord. Perhaps the thought of this final act of love kept them going during the long hours of the Sabbath.

The effect of Jesus' death on the disciples and the women must have been devastating. On top of their grief (for none of them had grasped Jesus' earlier words that he would rise again), they knew that after the Sabbath, they would be hunted down as followers of Jesus. They met behind locked doors, and dared not risk going out into the streets.

Then came Sunday morning, the day after the Sabbath. Very early, while it was still dark, at least six women made their way to the garden tomb where Jesus had been laid, bringing with them spices and ointments for his anointing. There was Mary Magdalene, Mary the wife of Cleopas, Salome (Jesus' aunt), Johanna, wife of Chuza, and at least two other women whose names are not given.

As they walked through the streets of Jerusalem in the darkness of that early morning, they discussed how they would roll the heavy stone away. Approaching the tomb, they saw, to their amazement, that the stone had already been rolled away! The women were nonplussed and stood there, not quite knowing what to do. Mary Magdalene immediately ran back through the city to tell Peter and John about the stone.

Let's pause for a moment to consider the events which occurred that morning, and then during the day. Matthew tells us (28:1–15) that:

- There was a great earthquake. This was the second earthquake in three days. (Verse 1)
- The soldiers guarding the tomb during the night after the Sabbath (early Sunday morning) were suddenly aghast to see an angel appear from heaven and roll back the stone and sit on it. (Verse 2)
- The incredulous soldiers were terrified at the sight of this angel who shone with the brightness of lightning, wearing clothes of glistering

white. To the soldiers, already nervous, and in the darkness of pre-dawn, this would be terrifying. (Verse 3)
• In their stark terror, the soldiers collapsed unconscious (Verse 4)

All this occurred before dawn and before the women arrived at the tomb.

The women now arrive. They didn't see the angel outside, but they did see that the stone had been rolled away. (Mark 16:4). They were very frightened. After Mary Magdalene had left to run and tell Peter and John about the stone, the remaining women ventured to look inside the tomb. They saw two young men, clothed in white, sitting in the tomb. These angels (for this is what they were), told the women not to be frightened, but to go and tell the disciples that Jesus had risen from the dead.

All this was too much for the frightened women, and they fled out of the tomb and out of the garden, back through the city to tell the disciples about their mind-boggling experience.

Just after they had left the garden, Peter, John and Mary Magdalene came running to the tomb. Peter and John apparently arrived before Mary, and they, too, went inside, but saw only the burial clothes in which Jesus had been wrapped, lying in the tomb. But they did not see the angels. The angels appeared to the women only.

Peter and John left the tomb, but Mary stayed there alone, crying. After a few minutes, she, too, looked inside the tomb, and there were the two angels, visible again! "Woman", they said, "Why are you weeping?" In Mary's tearful reply to them we glimpse her heartbreak and anguish, "Because they have taken away my Lord, and I do not know where they have laid him."

"They have taken away my Lord ..." How she loved her Lord. Let's not miss the personal feeling she had for her Lord, "My Lord". We, too, must think of him as "My Lord", with the same devotion as Mary felt as she tried to find out where they had taken him.

She looked around and saw a man standing behind her. She took him to be the gardener. He said, "Woman, why are you weeping? Whom do you seek?" Can we imagine the gentleness in Jesus' voice as he spoke to Mary? He knew what she had done for him by being with him at the foot of the cross during his long hours of agony and struggle. He knew she had helped lay him to rest in this tomb. And now she had returned with the intention of ministering to him as the final act of her love for him.

"Sir, if you have carried him away, tell me where you have laid him and I will take him away." Mary, little Mary, how would you take away his body? She could never carry him alone. The practicality of this never dawned on her. All that mattered to her was her love for him.

"Mary."

Just one word. Mary's heart must have almost stopped with shock and disbelief. She knew instantly that it was Jesus. "Rabboni!.", she gasped, and flung her arms around him. "Do not hold me", said Jesus, "for I have not yet ascended to the Father …"

So it was that faithful Mary was the first to see the risen Lord. He came to her first.

Meanwhile, the other women had reached the disciples and told them the message of the two angels. The disciples took no notice of the women. Luke says that "the report seemed nonsense to them. They did not believe the women."

As the day unfolded, Jesus appeared to three other people. First, to Peter, privately. What a meeting that would be, after Peter's denial and subsequent heartbreak! We don't know what Jesus said to Peter, or what Peter said to Jesus.

Then he appeared to Cleopas and his companion, who could well have been Mary, his wife, although we can't be certain of that. It had been Mary the wife of Cleopas, with Mary Magdalene, who had been so faithful at the cross and the tomb. Whilst the authorised version of the Bible speaks of "two men" on the road to Emmaus, the Greek words mean "O foolish ones", which could have meant either two men or a man and a woman, one of whom was Cleopas.

Did Jesus deliberately choose to appear first to those who had been so close to him, and so devoted to him? First, Mary Magdalene, second, Peter, and third, Mary the wife of Cleopas.

Then, that same evening, the ten disciples (Thomas was not with them) were gathered together behind locked doors. By now, they were beginning to realise that the women had been right. An astonished Peter had arrived and reported seeing and talking to the Lord! Now Cleopas and his companion came knocking at the door with the astounding news that they, too, had seen Jesus and had even eaten a meal with him!

As if that wasn't enough, as they told each other this amazing and almost unbelievable news, suddenly, there was Jesus amongst them. "Shalom", he said calmly. "Peace to you." What an impact he would have! No wonder Luke writes, "They were startled and frightened and thought he was a spirit."

But it really was Jesus, who talked with them and showed them the marks in his hands and feet and side, and who ate some fish with them.

Eight days later, he appeared to them again, and this time, Thomas was with them. Then a few weeks later, he appeared to seven of the disciples beside the Sea of Galilee and provided breakfast for them. This was his third appearance to them as a group.

Shortly after that, he met with five hundred brethren — very likely in the hills of Galilee. To get five hundred followers of Jesus together was a major triumph of careful planning. It couldn't take place in any town because the Jewish authorities would have promptly arrested all of them.

One by one, two by two, these faithful brethren made their unobtrusive way to an isolated spot in the hills, and there, to their great joy, they met their risen Lord. These men became the basis of the newly forming Christian church. Under the leadership of the apostles, they were to go out and preach a risen and alive Jesus, the Christ. They had seen him, and talked with him personally. They were five hundred personal witnesses that he was alive.

These brethren were essential to the work of preaching the gospel in those early days:

> "Go and make disciples of all nations, baptising them in the name of the Father and of the Son and of the Holy Spirit, teaching them to observe all that I have commanded you ..." (Matthew 28:19–20)

So important were these brethren in this work, that twenty-four years later, Paul wrote of them, and obviously knew them, for he said, "Then he appeared to more than five hundred brethren at one time, most of whom are still alive, though some have fallen asleep."

Shortly before Jesus ascended to heaven, he appeared to his own brother, James, who by then, along with his other brothers, had accepted Jesus as their Lord and Saviour.

Finally, at the end of forty days, Jesus and his apostles stood once more on the Mount of Olives, and seemingly without any warning, he began to rise into the air, and as they watched, gazing into heaven, a cloud took him out of their sight.

As the eleven apostles watched, they became aware of two men beside them in white robes. Surely these were the two angels who had sat within the tomb forty days earlier, and had appeared to the women. Now, for the first time, they revealed themselves to the men. "This same Jesus", they told the apostles, "will come again in the same way as you saw him go into heaven."

So ended these stupendous forty days when our risen Lord appeared to, and talked, with those who loved him.

From then on, news of the dramatic fact that Jesus, the Son of God, who had died and was now alive, was the match that kindled the fire of Christianity around the world. His death and resurrection opened up the way to our Heavenly Father through the new covenant. As Paul wrote to the new Christian believers at Colossae:

> "He has delivered us from the dominion of darkness and transferred us to the Kingdom of His beloved Son, in whom we have redemption, the forgiveness of sins." (Colossians 1:13–14)

We rejoice that Jesus is alive, and now sits in immortality beside his Father in heaven.

We rejoice, too, that we know he will return to rule the earth with righteousness, peace and justice, when sin will ultimately be destroyed and when illness, trouble, suffering and death will be no more.

Jesus himself told John, in Revelation 7:16–17, that his saints who will be granted immortality will:

"... hunger no more, neither thirst any more; the sun shall not strike them, nor any scorching heat. For the Lamb in the midst of the throne will be their shepherd, and he will guide them to springs of living water; and God will wipe away every tear from their eyes."

And so we shall always be with Jesus.